Attachment-Based Teaching

NORTON BOOKS IN EDUCATION

Attachment-Based Teaching

CREATING A TRIBAL CLASSROOM

Louis Cozolino

W. W. NORTON & COMPANY
NEW YORK • LONDON

For information about permission to reproduce selections from this book, write
to Permissions, W. W. Norton & Company, Inc., 500 Fifth Avenue,
New York, NY 10110

For information about special discounts for bulk purchases, please contact
W. W. Norton Special Sales at specialsales@wwnorton.com or 800-233-4830

Manufacturing by Quad Graphics, Fairfield
Production manager: Leeann Graham

Library of Congress Cataloging-in-Publication Data

ISBN: 978-0-393-70904-9 (pbk.)

W. W. Norton & Company, Inc., 500 Fifth Avenue, New York, N.Y. 10110
www.wwnorton.com
W. W. Norton & Company Ltd., Castle House, 75/76 Wells Street,
London W1T 3QT

1 2 3 4 5 6 7 8 9 0

This book is dedicated to my friend and teacher Alex Caldwell.

Contents

PART IV TAPPING INTO PRIMITIVE SOCIAL INSTINCTS

Acknowledgments

I would like to thank Deborah Malmud of W. W. Norton for her encouragement and guidance during the writing of this book. Special thanks go also to Erin Santos for her many intellectual and editorial contributions to the text. Thank you to my colleagues at Pepperdine, especially Diana Beck for her assistance with the manuscript and to Ramy Rizkallah for his never-ending technical support. Special thanks also go to my colleagues Peter Murphy and Daniel Franklin for their belief in this work and for helping me expose it to a wider audience. Thanks also go to Lisa Shapiro and Megan Marcus for their encouragement and contributions to this book.

Attachment-Based Teaching

An invasion of armies can be resisted,
but not an idea whose time has come.

Victor Hugo

PART I

The Social Brain

CHAPTER 1

The Power of Attachment

Every child needs a champion.

Rita Pierson

In this first chapter I lay the foundation for what is to come by defining and discussing four core principles—tribes, secure attachment, neuroplasticity, and work-arounds—which serve as the center of an attachment-based classroom. But first I describe some of the assumptions that our present education system is based on and why it fails so many students.

The story of education that I am about to tell is based on how the human brain evolved to learn. It is a story grounded in the deep history of our species and reflected in our religious traditions, politics, and the way we care for one another. It is the story of us.

Evolution by natural selection was Charles Darwin's way of explaining how animals change over many generations to adapt to the changing demands of the environment. According to his theory, diversity among animals, combined with selective reproduction, dictated how the necks of giraffes grew longer to reach the leaves on high branches and how the shape of hummingbird beaks came to reflect the shape of the flowers that hold their food.

Darwin's theory can also be applied to how our brains have evolved. After all, if necks and beaks can go through adaptive changes, why not brains? It seems clear that human brains have changed in some important ways over the thousands of generations that came before we were born. The most significant of these changes may be that brains evolved into social organs. This means that the adaptations driving natural selection have shifted from the physical to the social environment. This now means that those that relate best, survive best.

For most of the last 100,000 years, humans have lived in small bands of closely related people generally referred to as tribes. *Tribes* were our social environments, and individuals with greater social skills were more likely to reproduce. It is within these small groups that the ways in which we attach and learn became interwoven. Based on the relationship between learning and attachment, we can enhance education by simulating the social and emotional elements of the groups in which our brains evolved to learn.

A *tribe* is a group of individuals that are tied together by shared time, familiarity, affection, and common purpose. Tribes were the social environments to which our brains adapted over countless generations. A tribe is a super-organism, meaning that individuals in it have a better chance surviving together than separately. It also means that support for the tribe often surpasses individual needs, which results in caretaking, self-sacrifice, and other forms of altruistic behavior.

One Size Fits All

We shape our buildings, and afterwards our buildings shape us.
                                        Winston Churchill

Teaching was traditionally carried out by close relatives and tribal elders, a custom that was largely lost during the Industrial Revolution. Society was so bedazzled by thousands of products flowing off assembly lines that we began to educate children in the same way. We imagined waves of students flowing from schools into offices and factories to create even more products. The fact that humans evolved to attach to and learn from one another was lost.

While the challenges of contemporary education are many, three stand out as particularly relevant in light of what we now know about the human brain. First, schools, like factories, usually assume the input of consistent raw materials. Students, however, are unique. They come from all classes and cultures with a wide range of social, emotional, and cognitive abilities (and disabilities). Yet schools are mandated to teach all students using the same methods, materials, and standards. Regardless of whether students are prepared and able to learn or whether their teachers have the time, training, and resources to educate them, success is measured by standardized tests—the quality control measure of industrial education.

Second, teachers are not interchangeable cogs in a factory machine that engage in the rapid repetition of specific behaviors. Teachers, like their students, are unique individuals, and it is the nature, quality, and uniqueness of teacher-student relationships that create possibilities for learning. This is especially true for children with challenges, who require greater flexibility in establishing relationships and receiving the curriculum. As you will see in the chapters to come, this basic mismatch between industrial education and the process of human learning contains the seeds of both student dropout and teacher burnout.

Third, unlike factories, we are uncertain of the final product we are aiming for. Education is supposed to prepare young people for the future—but what future? The people currently making decisions about curriculum were educated before the Internet, personal computers, or even answering machines. The world is changing so quickly that it is hard to know what knowledge and skills children will need to have twenty or even ten years from now. In the absence of clear goals, it is nearly impossible to gauge the true effectiveness of a curriculum. When test performance is the measure of success, the good student is one who can store and recall facts with minimal distraction and complaint. Such a student is rewarded for information retention and "citizenship" (compliance), but is this a formula for future success?

Teachers are tasked with the job of engaging with, attaching to, and teaching children in the real world. Students are not uniform raw materials but a diverse collection of living, breathing human beings with complex personalities and life stories. When you remove uniform materials and clear outcomes, you need creative teachers who can bring their humanity to work and who can make decisions on an individual basis. Teaching comprises a complex set of skills, which is very dissimilar to working on an assembly line.

If we are going to move forward, we will have to admit that a one-size-fits-all model of education is doomed to fail many, if not most, students. While we're at it, let's also admit that although there is plenty of rhetoric about how to prepare students for the future, we have little solid information. We have no idea whether to limit or encourage access to social networking, computer games, television, and other forms of media. We don't know if these activities are hurting their intellectual and interpersonal development or better preparing them for the world ahead.

Will reading the great books, studying ancient philosophy, or knowing the nuts and bolts of mathematics be of any help to our children in the future? Should we foster open-mindedness and freethinking or push the accumulation of facts and the use of search engines? Should the focus of education be social responsibility, *empathy*, and *mindfulness* as multiculturalism becomes more of an everyday reality? Our feelings about these issues are as strong as our knowledge is weak—I certainly have my own biases and beliefs—but no one has the answers.

Empathy is an idea you develop about the experience of others based on the emotions you witness them having, the context they are in, and the emotions evoked in you. It is always important to remember that empathy is a hypothesis about another person that needs verification from that person.

Mindfulness is a term used to describe the ability to reflect on inner experience. The focus of this reflection can be the stream of our conscious thoughts, physical sensations, or emotional experiences and the images they may evoke.

Science and Education

Education is a progressive discovery of our own ignorance.
                                                      Will Durant

Since their creation, America's public schools have served as a tool of cultural homogenization. It was long ago hoped that a successful school would polish members of cultural minorities into "true" Americans by converting them to the values and behaviors of the northern European majority. This required a requisite level of cultural shame, an abandonment of traditional values, and an idealization of becoming Anglicized. In many ways, the culture has shifted from Anglocentrism to one of cultural pluralism with the goal of being integrated, equal, and diverse. Pluralism, with all of its advantages, brings an array of new challenges to the classroom.

Every school is embedded within an existing community that connects hundreds of families through their children. The strength of these connections depends upon a sense of partnership resting on a shared commitment to education. In a safe community with strong families that value education, a competent teacher can do a good job. In a dangerous community with few resources, fragmented families, and an indifference to education, a successful teacher has to be a superhero.

Today's inner-city schools present a far harsher reality for African American, Hispanic, and Asian American students than anything I ever encountered. The drugs, violence, and rage in today's schools would have seemed like an apocalyptic nightmare when I was a boy. Unfortunately, this nightmare is an everyday reality for countless children. We are now seeing the effects of these horrific environments on how children think about themselves and the roles they come to play in society. The current system is not equipped to support all of the diverse needs of its students.

As the problems worsen, educators have turned to science for answers. Millions are spent on iPads, Smart Boards, and stimulant medications, while training teachers in nurturing social-emotional development is rarely discussed. My contention is that the solutions to many of the problems of education are not technical but deeply human in nature.

By relying on science, we have repeatedly underestimated the inherent wisdom in culture and human experience, which has been shaped over millions of years. Here is a good example. Existing tribal communities have been discovered that practice scattered farming where, instead of a single field, a farmer may have a dozen or more small and widely dispersed gardens. This exasperated well-meaning Westerners, who lamented the amount of time wasted in walking from garden to garden each day—more time than they actually spent tending to their crops. Attempts at enlightening the farmers with modern farming techniques proved fruitless. However, subsequent analysis revealed that although scattered gardening yielded less overall production, it also resulted in no year with total crop failure. In other words, the farmer's survival depended upon maintaining this less efficient method.

The farmer's wisdom had been shaped by thousands of years of natural selection. Families who farmed in this scattered manner—different elevations, sides of the mountain, proximity to water—had the greatest probability of survival. The windstorms, floods, droughts, or foraging animals that may have destroyed one or more gardens never ruined all of them. This may sound surprisingly familiar to those of us who diversify our investment portfolios and avoid putting all of our eggs in one basket. The innate wisdom embodied in this tribal practice was as invisible to modern scientists as the value of secure student-teacher attachment is to most modern educational theorists.

What Does Science Have to Offer?

I change my mind when the facts change. What do you do?

John Maynard Keynes

Teachers rightfully question the value of experts who pepper standard educational theory with words like *neuron, cortex,* and *synapse.* But let's not throw out the baby with the bathwater. We have learned a few things, including the fact that proper nutrition has a measurable impact on memory and learning, as do

sleep and physical activity. Adolescents do have different biological clocks that affect their sleep-wake cycles and result in
different learning abilities at different times of the day. Also,
cognitive science has demonstrated that humans tend to remember better when information is presented in particular ways and
at a certain pace (for a biologist's perspective see Zull, 2002).

Despite the potential benefits of these scientific findings,
none of them address the failure of the system as a whole. This
is because teaching is an essentially human endeavor, ill matched
to Western scientific methodologies applied within a model of
mass production.

All too often, those who promote some brand of scientific
learning assume our brains are separate organs that live in a
vacuum. This leads them to assume that brains can be understood in isolation and that what is learned in the laboratory
can be directly applied in the classroom. However, our social
brains reside within an interwoven matrix of relationships and
the realities of day-to-day survival. Despite being overlooked by
scientists who study learning in the laboratory, a student's ability to learn is deeply impacted by the quality of his or her
attachment to teachers and peers.

Secure attachment is the ability to be soothed by others and
to experience safety through proximity. In the classroom,
secure attachments to teachers and other students optimize the ability to learn. This biological connection has
been shaped by evolution within brain networks dedicated
to learning, stress, and social relationships.

What is missing in essentially all science-based education
theories is the recognition that the human brain is a social
organ of adaptation. The brain has evolved to interact with the
environment for the sake of survival. As a social organ, human

brains have evolved to be linked to and learn from other brains in the context of significant relationships. Data from social neuroscience, cultural anthropology, and biochemistry all support the theory that our brains evolved to learn from caring and compassionate teachers who know us well and who are invested in our well-being.

There is no substitute for the instincts of bright, dedicated, and caring teachers—these are the real experts. Scientists should study the work of these teachers, figure out why they are successful, and explore what their success tells us about how brains learn. What I am attempting to do is just that—to use science to more fully understand why successful teachers are successful, which brain systems they are tapping into, and how they stimulate *neuroplasticity* and learning.

Neuroplasticity is the ability of the nervous system to change in response to experience. The brain has been shaped by evolution to adapt and readapt to an ever-changing world. In other words, the brain exists to learn, remember, and apply what it has learned. Learning is dependent upon modifications of the brain's chemistry and architecture in a process called **neural plasticity**. Neural plasticity reflects the ability of neurons to change both their structure and their relationships to one another for the purpose of learning based on new experiences.

The Path Into a Closed Mind Is an Open Heart

True friendship can afford true knowledge.

Henry David Thoreau

Deep in prehistory, early learning took place in pairs or in small groups of related individuals with a "curriculum" guided by day-to-day survival. For a hundred thousand years, anatomically modern humans evolved in small tribal communities, held together by family relationships, cooperation, and common rituals. The interdependence of group members continued to interweave their brains until tribes were shaped into superorganisms. Thinking of the brain in this way is supported by thousands of studies that attest to the impact of relationships on health, well-being, and learning.

The neurolinguist John Schulman once told me that the best way to learn a second language is to fall in love with someone who only speaks that language. Beyond providing motivation and practice, the neurochemistry of love and attachment stimulates the neuroplasticity of learning. Perhaps this can be turned into a more general statement—the best way to learn in school is to fall in love with your teacher. It was certainly true for me.

How can a classroom stimulate *primitive social instincts*, neuroplasticity, and learning? We have learned by studying tribal communities that exist today that social life is shaped by cooperation, equality, and service-based leadership. Cooperation, grounded in kinship and common interests, is reinforced through obvious survival benefits, especially when resources are scarce or when faced with a common enemy. Equality and a sense of fairness within a tribe make each member feel valued while increasing their commitment to the tribe. Finally, leadership is earned through skills and services provided to other members of the tribe. In the classroom, authority is based on service to students and the value a teacher brings to the class.

Primitive social instincts were shaped at the beginning of the evolution of social animals to promote bonding, attachment, and maternal caretaking. They were later used to connect families, clans, and small tribes. These are the instincts that drive us to self-sacrifice, to acts of charity, and to give so much of ourselves to our children and others we love. Primitive social instincts are primarily driven by biochemical reactions that are triggered in situations of parenting, mating, and group formation.

In contrast to traditional tribal values, leadership within industrial societies and educational systems is based on competition, individual success, obedience, and power over others. This means larger groups are organized via social hierarchies, inequality, and dominance. Our brains are wired to resist and rebel against coercion, submission, and a lack of fairness. This is why cooperative groups survive and why unfair practices in any group plant the seeds of discord and failure. The focus of this book is to guide you to create a tribal classroom so that you can leverage these primitive social instincts for the benefit of your students.

Reflection Box: Cooperative Leadership

Imagine taking this attitude in relation to your students and investing more time in exploring how the class can share leadership responsibilities with you. Are there ways that you can include your students in decision making that promote cooperation, democracy, equality, and fairness that will encourage tribal connections and enhance primitive social instincts?

While Western culture has changed a great deal during the last 5,000 years, our instincts, biochemistry, and neural networks that evolved in the context of tribal life are essentially unchanged. Considerable evidence supports the idea that those who best avoid the downside of modern industrial culture are those who join or create tribes. From churchgoers, to sports fans, to gang members, the drive to join some version of a tribe and the benefits derived from membership are undeniable. It appears that at this point in our evolution, we still have one foot firmly planted in our tribal past.

The tribal values of mutual respect, cooperation, and caring that shaped our social brains for countless generations have been largely factored out of the modern cultural equation. However, the most successful institutions appear to be those that are able to integrate the instinctual imperatives of our tribal brains into the structures of contemporary hierarchical organizations. The accommodations of tribal instincts within large institutions, referred to as *work-arounds*, enhance large-group functioning by activating primitive social instincts (Richerson & Boyd, 2006). An example of such a work-around is social situations that encourage teachers get to know each other as people beyond their role as professional colleagues. The personal connections made in these situations, especially if they are emotional and genuine, serve to move the faculty and the school in the direction of a tribe.

A ***work-around*** is a strategy to activate small-group dynamics, promote primitive social instincts, and secure attachment within larger organizations. Good examples include sports teams, military platoons, and a group of people working on a project for which they have commitment and passion.

The most successful modern institutions may well be those that have found a way to integrate and leverage the instincts of our primitive social brains. One example is a factory that is organized around small production groups for the purpose of enhanced identification with the product and improved quality control. Others include military hierarchies and sports teams that encourage intense ritualistic bonding in small subgroups as they prepare for combat or competition. These work-arounds are accommodations to tribal instincts within large hierarchies. Teachers that can create, maintain, and utilize these work-arounds to enhance emotional involvement, motivation, and teamwork will almost certainly create a more successful learning group.

Suggested Work-Arounds

The following are some suggested work-arounds that support translating the theory of tribal education into practice.

Keep Classrooms and Schools as Small as Possible

The interpersonal distance and emotional numbing that is our natural reaction to large numbers of people need to be taken out of the educational equation. A school needs to be a small town, not a large city. It should be unthinkable to make believe that someone you are passing by doesn't exist. If a small school is not a current option, consider dividing up a school into smaller tribes that you can call anything you like. Divide a school into floors or wings or points on the compass, develop an identity for each, and create programming that gives these tribes a sense of belonging. It will also make them feel like members of the school as a whole. They can compete in sports and community fund-raising, or sponsor social events for one another—think of sororities and fraternities where a student has a dual loyalty to the school and the house. This can be cultivated in larger schools. Students can also be arranged into smaller tribes in a large classroom.

Create Sufficient Time for Bonding

Meeting times should be established throughout the week, and lunches should be long to allow both students and teachers time to bond, exchange experiences, and focus on shared projects. Students, teachers, and staff should also spend time together outside of the learning environment to deepen their connections to one another. Building a tribe takes time.

Decentralize the Class by Creating Learning Cooperatives

Break students up into thoughtfully formed smaller groups that work together to solve problems. Factors like personality styles, strengths, and experience should all be considered to maximize group success.

Community Service

In line with finding a worthy cause, community service should be one of the centerpieces of school and classroom activities. Done properly, these are ways of engaging hearts, minds, and bodies in the processes of reaching out to a broader world. No one, no matter how much they may be suffering, can't be helped by helping others. One of my teachers once told me to remember, "Whenever you are confused about who you are, serve others and you will find out." We all need to understand the hard work we are summoned to by compassion. This also creates a common goal for our students, which facilitates bonding.

Worthy Challenges and Meaningful Work

Find ways for all students to engage in work that has meaning and value to the community. These projects can be tied to community service and fund-raising for school or community projects. Don't protect children from the real world—they need enough of a challenge to stimulate their brain to learn.

Focus on Current Events With Human Interest Stories

The world is the best source of learning material. Things are in the news because they are relevant to human experience. Violent crimes are invitations to discussions about gun control, racial strife, mental illness, traumatic stress, and so on. Terrorist attacks can lead to political, geographical, and religious explorations. Students may also feel comfortable sharing personal experiences that relate to these larger issues.

Meaningful and Emotional Participation by Parents, Grandparents, and Caring Others

Involve as many parents as possible to expand the knowledge base within the classroom and to maximize the classroom and the school's connection with the community. Don't have parents just show up; include them in planning and thinking through the assignments and challenges that will be presented to the students. Don't assume teachers will be naturally good at this type of community organizing—principals should give them the type of training and support they will need to be successful. However, if these resources are not offered at your school, numerous resources are available from nonprofits, publishers, and other teachers.

The success of these creative uses of our ancient instincts within a more modern framework leaves no doubt of their continued relevance to human experience. As you will see, teachers who are able to tap into the primitive social instincts of their students through attachment relationships and by structuring tribal classrooms are able to succeed in seemingly impossible educational situations.

Exercise 1: Going Tribal

Creating a tribal classroom includes broad participation, respect, and democratic decision making. One easy way to start is to begin thinking about how to include students in class structure and preparation.

Students are aware of some of the issues discussed in this chapter, but they are seldom, if ever, encouraged to talk openly about them in class. The fact that they talk a great deal about what they like and dislike about school with friends is an indication both of its importance and the fact that they need to feel safe to open up about these issues.

Although taking responsibility for the curriculum and teaching methods is at the heart of our training, consider building the class in collaboration with your students. Co-constructing the class as the first group assignment will set the foundation for a tribal classroom. Imagine starting out the school year with these three discussion questions and the formulation of a class contract.

*1. What have been your favorite classes, teachers, and
learning experiences, in or out of school?*

Depending on age and experience, students will mention everything from an art class, to karate lessons, to a trip to the zoo. Once everyone has shared, work with the class to pull out common themes and write them on the board. Themes might include being physically active, teachers with a good sense of humor, learning something particularly interesting, or anything involving pizza. Allow humor to be part of the process, with things like pizza being woven in with the more serious suggestions. What will emerge in this discussion are those things that motivate students to engage in the learning process. Once the themes have been articulated, begin an analysis of the factors that made them memorable with questions like the following:

2. What did you like about it? What made it so special?
How did it make you feel?

Once again, begin to discern common themes and write them on the board. Good examples might be "feeling that the teacher liked me," "time flew by without me realizing it," or "it felt safe to make mistakes." What will emerge during this discussion are the basic themes of tribal learning that children instinctively understand. They will describe, in their own language, what turns their brains on and off and the type of environments that optimize learning. The next step, application, is the hardest, and it begins by asking the following general question.

3. How can we take the best aspects of these past
experiences and build them into the learning experience
we are about to create together?

The basic goal is to recognize what stimulates learning and how the entire class can contribute in making the class the best experience possible. Different people learn differently, and clusters of individuals can come together to create learning experiences that work best for them. Start by listing some of the required topics to be studied during the year; then describe some of the ways in which they can be approached. Finally, open the floor to these and other ideas leading to organizing how the class will be structured. When possible, incorporate student suggestions and preferences into your lesson plan. This mirrors the activity of a tribal council making decisions that maximize benefit and minimize suffering. The end result of this process is drafting a contract.

4. Drafting a contract.

The tribal contract can contain anything that the class decides on from time spent on homework, to community projects they would like to participate in, to agreeing to create a supportive and nonshaming class. It should also include issues like commitment to doing homework, getting together outside of class for social and community service activities, and study groups. Drafting the contract as a group, having everyone sign it, and distributing copies to all the students, their parents, and any other stakeholders makes the commitment to the tribe public. It is the tribe's flag and coat of arms, and it solidifies the challenge the tribe is about to engage in. The contract can be established at the beginning of the school year and revisited on a regular basis for readjustment as new learning and insights occur. The following are some ideas to get you thinking about what you might want to include in a classroom contract.

5. Suggested classroom contract.

Below is a sample classroom contract. Feel free to use the pieces that fit your classroom. Other aspects won't apply to your students. Instead, you can add additional information for specific challenges that your students may face during the year. If you already have a classroom contract, consider adding information specific to tribal classrooms.

Classroom Contract

Teacher's Commitment to the Students

1. I will work with the students to decide the best learning techniques for the class. Every student will have a say in how the materials are presented and taught.

2.   I will have office hours after school every Thursday when students can stop by to discuss personal experiences, classroom problems, or other issues. I will also be available every Tuesday during lunch.

3.   I will provide a weekly activity to reduce stress and anxiety. This will include mindfulness techniques, group sharing, or team-building exercises.

4.   I will be available to students even after the school year has ended. I am committed to my students, and I will be a resource to them as long as possible.

Students' Commitment to the Class

1.   We agree to take care of each other. There will be no ridicule or shaming in or out of the classroom. We will also let the teacher know if any bullying occurs outside the classroom.

2.   We will meet weekly with our study groups outside the classroom. In these groups, we will work together on various projects or homework assignments. We will also help each other with any difficult subjects. If necessary, we will reach out to the teacher or our parents for additional help.

3.   Every week, five students will present current events. These events will be related to our community or the school. The presenting students will then lead the discussion on how these events relate to larger social issues.

4.   We will reach out to the teacher when there is a problem. We will let our teacher know if we are struggling academically, socially, or at home.

Parents' Commitment to the Classroom

1.   We will make ourselves available to our children and the teacher.

2.   Whenever necessary, we will provide additional assistance at home for assignments or group projects.

3. We will be involved in the classroom and do our best to assist the teacher as needed.

4. If a problem arises at home, we will notify the teacher as soon as possible.

5. We will prioritize our child's education.

Classroom Expectations

1. When possible, decisions will be made in a democratic fashion. The class will collectively decide how to spend free time. The class will also vote to decide the best way to tackle new subjects and projects.

2. The teacher will present two or three lesson plans before starting a new subject. The students will then vote on which lesson plan to utilize in class.

3. Once a month, the class will be able to devote extra time to enhancing our classroom community. Students will have the opportunity to stay late after class to address any challenges, improve the classroom, or engage in relationship-building exercises.

4. Throughout the year, we will all work toward our collective class goal. Based on the class vote, this year we will raise money to donate to a local charity.

5. All class conflicts will be dealt with as a group. Students will elect a student to be ombudsperson every month. The ombudsperson will work to gather information about any conflicts that arise in class. The conflict will then be presented to the classroom. Collectively, the students and teacher will determine how to fairly resolve the conflict.

6. This contract will be revised each semester as necessary.

By signing this agreement, the students, parents, and teacher agree to the terms above. Additionally, everyone in this classroom will work to create a healthy, calm, and kind learning environment so that everyone can succeed.

CHAPTER 2

Our Social Brains

The more original a discovery, the more obvious it seems afterward.

Arthur Koestler

Relationships are our natural habitat and the drive to belong is a fundamental human motivation. From birth until death, each of us needs others to help us feel safe, seek us out, and show interest in discovering who we are. Regardless of age, it is vital for us to feel a part of, participate in, and contribute to our various tribes. This is as true for principals, teachers, and school board members as it is for our students. Let's look at how the brain evolved into a social organ, shaped by the tribal environment to which it had to adapt for thousands of generations.

Western ways of thinking are biased toward the importance of the individual organism. Thus, our science mostly examines single organs, individual bodies, and isolated minds. In the same vein, our educational systems encourage competition, test scores, and individual accomplishments. As much as we may want to adhere to the notion of the single self, humans have evolved as social creatures and are constantly influencing each other's behaviors, thoughts, and emotions. Without mutually stimulating interactions, people (and the neurons within our brains) wither and die. In neurons, this process is called apoptosis, which is caused by a lack of attachment and stimulation. In humans, it is called failure to thrive, depression, or dying of a broken heart.

Forgetting that we are social animals can have tragic results. Take, for example, the way in which physicians responded to the high mortality rates of children in orphanages early in the last century. Assuming that infections from microorganisms were to blame, they separated children from one another and kept contact with adults to a minimum. Sadly, children continued to die at alarming rates. It wasn't until attachment researchers suggested that children be held and played with by consistent caretakers and allowed to interact with one another that their survival rates improved. What better evidence is there that the brain is a social organ requiring human contact as much as oxygen and glucose?

Insecure attachment is the inability to be soothed and comforted by others. Thought to be the result of unpredictable and/or anxiety-provoking interactions with caretakers, individuals with insecure attachments do not gain a predictable sense of safety in relationships with others.

When educators focus on curricular content and test performance instead of student-teacher connections, they are guilty of a similar blind spot as these physicians. It is time to improve education by rethinking it from a social and interactive perspective. Let's begin by thinking about the brain in a historical context.

How Human Brains Changed Into Social Organs

Those who have learned to collaborate and improvise most effectively have prevailed.

Attributed to Charles Darwin

For most of the last 100,000 years, anatomically modern humans lived in bands and tribes that became woven into social super-organisms. Consistent contact, high levels of interdependence, and group solidarity characterized these bands. In the absence of outside authority, group norms were shaped by the demands of day-to-day survival and enforced by tribal culture. Lacking a rigid hierarchy and assigned leaders, members worked together through cooperation and consensus building in reaction to everyday situations and especially in times of war and famine.

It is likely that the most viable tribes were more collaborative, flexible, and inclusive of all their members. These tendencies would improve a tribe's reaction to changing situations while maximizing the contribution of all of its members. Respect and leadership status would be earned through fairness, generosity, and attention to the well-being of the tribe.

It was within this interpersonal environment that natural selection shaped our primary social instincts. This may be why we are not able to tolerate more than minimal coercion, injustice, and a lack of fairness toward others. As we see in the contemporary world, repressive and unfair social arrangements are less stable and ultimately drive people to revolt. Perhaps contemporary humans have such a low tolerance for inequality because we were programmed long ago to resist unfair and excessive social control, as it was associated with tribal failure. To this day, highly functional and long-lived countries and institutions manage to create generally accepted customs and fair laws. Unfair leadership in the classroom will have the same negative effects on students as unfair administrators have on teachers.

Most important for our current focus is that in small-scale societies, education is not a separate activity but an aspect of everyday life. Teaching in tribal societies is performed by biologically related, caring, and deeply invested elders. Teachers and students are bound together by affection, kinship, and mutual survival. Teachers were likely "elected" in an organic way as members of the tribe gravitated to them based on their ability to teach. Tribal teachers were also well aware that they would eventually come to depend on their students for survival.

The physical setting of the *tribal classroom* was the natural environment where students and teachers joined together to gather food, solve problems, and defend the community against external attacks. The curriculum was guided by the practical tasks of day-to-day life and the evolving needs of the community. In these naturally occurring apprenticeships, learning was interwoven with the biochemistry of attachment. This is the primary reason why attachment enhances learning. Teachers re-create this type of environment by establishing bonds of affection with their students and tribal classrooms within modern schools.

A *tribal classroom* is inspired by what we believe to be the basic interpersonal dynamics of the small-scale groups that humans evolved in for hundreds of thousands of years. The assumption is that the more a classroom parallels the dynamics of these natural social systems, the more that attachment relationships and the social structure of the group will optimize neuroplasticity and learning.

Rapid Cultural Change

There is more to life than increasing its speed.

Mahatma Gandhi

To this day, many groups around the world adhere to traditional tribal structures and values. In contrast, Western culture has experienced a rapid shift from tribal to agricultural to industrial forms of society. While a thousand years is a long time for cultural evolution, it is the blink of an eye in terms of biological evolution; we still retain many of our primitive instincts. The disparity of our biological and cultural clocks has resulted in a dilemma—tribal brains navigating modern culture. In other words, we find ourselves in a world that is poorly matched with our biology and basic social instincts. In a way, we are all like Crocodile Dundee in the big city.

In contrast to tribal life, industrial society is characterized by larger groups, division of labor, and constant contact with strangers. Equality is replaced with dominance hierarchies based on discipline, obedience, and a lack of fairness. If you haven't already noticed, all of these circumstances cause stress and inhibit learning. See Table 2.1 for some of the basic differences between tribal and industrial societies.

TABLE 2.1 Tribal Versus Modern Society

The Tribe	Industrial Society
Small groups	Large groups
Cooperation	Individualism
Equality and Fairness	Dominance hierarchy
Democratic decision making	Imposed and enforced rules
Cohesiveness	Competition
Shared responsibilities	Unequal division of labor

The drive to belong to a tribe and the intense loyalties that it activates are undeniable. The increases in psychological well-being, longevity, and learning abilities also reflect how social connections are tied to our biochemistry and immunological systems. Perhaps some of the loneliness, alienation, and depression so common in modern society are the result of a fundamental mismatch between brain and culture. Those who cope best with these feelings find ways to be a member of a tribe within the broader society.

Thus, modern humans appear to have two sets of layered social instincts. The first is a set of primitive social instincts rooted in the blood connections of family and tribe, which we share with other mammals and primates. The second is a modern addition that connects us in larger groups based on more abstract loyalties. The evolution of these *modern social instincts* depended upon the emergence of higher brain networks required for concepts like America, Christianity, or democracy that are too abstract to experience directly.

The emotional power of our loyalty to larger groups and abstract principles is grounded in our brain's capacity to link them to the survival reflexes of our primitive social instincts. This provides us with the motivation to fight and die for beliefs and principles. In this way, the primitive reflexes of our social brains are utilized in the service of maintaining large institutions in the contemporary world.

Modern social instincts evolved from basic social instincts to allow us to form bonds and loyalty to larger groups based on abstract principles. The emergence of modern social instincts relied upon connecting abstract concepts of loyalty related to large groups and strangers to the biochemical processes of primitive social instincts.

Primitive Social Instincts and Emotional Nurturance

True teachers are bridges over which they invite their students to cross.

Nikos Kazantzakis

While some have called attachment building in the classroom an optional agenda, I would suggest that it is absolutely essential. It is of special importance in teaching students who are unable to learn due to past trauma, social-emotional challenges, and cultural disconnections. The universality of primitive social instincts allows teachers to speak the emotional language of students from any culture or background. The ability to reach our students, especially those that are struggling, is essential. Taking a close look at the work of teachers who are successful with highly challenging students reveals that the more the emotional climate of the classroom matches the characteristics of tribal life, the better students and teachers perform. These tribal classrooms are examples of work-arounds, where attachment and group cohesion serve to stimulate learning.

While our modern social instincts have their roots in primitive tribal bonding, these social instincts have their origin in mother-child bonding and attachment. This prolonged, intimate caretaking is the evolutionary cradle of the human social brain. For young children, survival doesn't depend on how fast we run, climb a tree, or tell the difference between edible and poisonous mushrooms. Rather, we survive based on our abilities to bond with our parents and detect the needs and intentions of those around us. If we are successful in relationships and become woven into the fabric of the tribe, we will get what we need to survive. When children do not feel accepted, they fear for their survival and are unable to learn.

Not only are we wired to connect with and learn from others, we are also wired to need others to treat us with respect, care, and compassion. The Golden Rule—"do unto others as you would have them do unto you"—is driven by a complex neurobiology of emotional attunement. On the other hand, the golden rule for industry—"those with the gold make the rules"—does not sit well with most of us.

In contemporary society, the real challenges are multitasking, balancing the demands of work and family, information management, and coping with stress. We need to maintain perspective, pick our battles carefully, and remain mindful of our needs and limitations in the midst of countless competing demands. What prepares us best for these challenges? In some ways, it is the same thing that prepared our ancient ancestors to survive in their world—nurturance and support—which play vital roles in the development and integration of the diverse brain systems.

When we raise and educate children, we are shaping their brains in ways that will either help or harm their ability to navigate their lives. Healthy early relationships allow us to think well of ourselves, trust others, regulate our emotions, and utilize our intellectual and emotional intelligence during decision making. These early experiences shape the networks of the *prefrontal cortex*. Decades of research findings across a variety of disciplines all point to the same conclusion: those who are nurtured best learn best and survive best.

The ***prefrontal cortex***, the front-most portion of our brains, plays a central role in the development of social skills, emotional regulation, and impulse control. As you can imagine, a well-functioning prefrontal cortex allows us to better navigate relationships, the emotional ups and downs of everyday life, and learning.

When children experience abuse, neglect, or abandonment, the tribe is communicating to them that they are not acceptable or accepted members. Nonloving behavior teaches children that the world is a dangerous place, and it warns them to avoid exploration, risk taking, or trusting others. They grow to have thoughts, states of mind, emotions, and immunological functioning that are inconsistent with physical and mental well-being. When a teacher is harsh, critical, dismissive, demoralized, or overly stressed, students attune to and embody these antilearning states of mind. All of this conscious and unconscious information is communicated to students and regulates their ability to learn.

The Social Synapse

All learning is understanding relationships.
                                          George Washington Carver

Within the brain, individual neurons are separated by small gaps called *synapses* that are inhabited by a variety of chemical substances. It is this chemical communication that stimulates each neuron to survive, grow, and to be sculpted by experience. In a parallel mechanism, our social behaviors traverse the *social synapse*. The messages we send one another are received by the senses and converted into electrochemical signals within the social networks of the receiver's brain.

Much of the communication across the social synapse is automatic and unconscious; these communications can be sent via facial expressions, body language, your tone of voice, and the words you use. This invisible link is vital in education because interactions in and out of the classroom either excite or inhibit the neural plasticity upon which learning depends. This supports something you have probably already experienced—you are always communicating with your students, even when you are silent.

A *synapse* is a space between two neurons across which chemical messengers transmit signals to other neurons. People also communicate across the *social synapse* via a wide variety of verbal and nonverbal messages.

When we interact with one another, we trigger our brains to grow. Thus, we all participate in the shaping of each other's brains. Teaching triggers these same neurobiological processes, optimizing plasticity and building new neural structures in the service of learning. We know that animals raised in enriched and challenging environments have larger brains, longer neurons, and more synapses. Effective teachers use their personalities, interpersonal skills, and teaching methods to create enriched physical, intellectual, and social environments that stimulate neural plasticity, enhance brain development, and optimize learning. Put in slightly different terms, teachers are neuroscientists who conduct experiments in the neuroplasticity of learning every day.

Supportive, encouraging, and caring relationships stimulate neural circuitry to learn. High-risk children and adolescents who have become successful learners often report that one or two adults took a special interest in them and became invested in their success. You have the opportunity to be that person every moment of every day. This underscores the fact that humans engage more effectively in brain-altering learning when they are face-to-face, mind-to-mind, and heart-to-heart with caring others. This is how learning occurs in tribes and in tribal classrooms, where teachers and classmates become a tribe.

Four Key Aspects of Learning

To the child . . . traumas are not experienced as events in life, but as
life defining.

Christopher Bollas

Keep these four things in mind when planning out your teaching: brains grow best (1) in the context of supportive relationships, (2) during low levels of stress and emotional arousal, (3) where there is a balanced focus on thinking and feeling, and (4) through the creative use of stories.

While teachers may focus on what they are teaching, evolutionary theory and social neuroscience suggests that it is who we are that regulates neuroplasticity and learning. Secure relationships trigger brain growth and regulate emotions in ways that enhance learning. A low level of stress—where the learner is attentive and motivated to learn—maximizes the biochemical processes that drive plasticity.

Consider that the activation of both thinking and feeling allows executive networks to better coordinate both right and left hemispheres in support of emotional intelligence. Stories are wonderful because they always contain both of these elements. They also support memory and emotional regulation, and serve as a guide for future behavior. If you deliver your subject matter with these four principles in mind, you will be creating a tribal work-around that will advance learning by leveraging our primitive social instincts. See the following box for a brief description of the four key aspects of learning.

Four Key Aspects of Learning

Safe and Trusting Relationships

The position of the teacher parallels that of a parent in building a child's brain. Both can support emotional regulation by providing a safe haven that supports the learning process. This support, balanced with an appropriate level of challenge, activates the proper balance of neurotransmitters to create the states of mind and brain that activate memory and learning.

Teacher-student attunement is especially important with at-risk students. The social brain takes into account what we are learning and whom we are learning it from. Teachers can provide safe, trusting relationships by addressing shame, increasing independence, and strengthening bonds. More information and exercises are in Chapters 3 and 4.

Low to Moderate States of Anxiety and Arousal

Learning is optimized during low to moderate states of arousal and turned off in high states of arousal. The brain shuts down neural plasticity at very low levels of arousal to conserve energy and at high levels of arousal to divert energy toward immediate survival. Successful learning requires a state of interest and curiosity with minimal anxiety. Stress in the learning environment, traumatic memories from past learning experiences, or high levels of tension in a student's life outside the classroom all impair learning by inhibiting the neuroplastic functions of the brain.

When chronically stressed and traumatized learners are confronted with new learning, they are often unable to activate neuroplastic processes without emotional scaffolding. In Chapter 4, I discuss various techniques to measure and cope with anxiety. We can check in with students by taking their anxiety pulse. We can also utilize humor to help reduce student anxiety.

Thinking and Feeling

During primate evolution, the left and right hemi-spheres became increasingly different, the left specialized for language and rational thought, the right for strong emotion and physical experience. Because they can inhibit each other, emotions impair reasoning while intellectual defenses cut us off from our feelings. The attention to both thinking and feeling enhances emotional regulation and problem solving.

Experiences that encourage critical thinking in emo-tionally salient situations enhance hemispheric integra-tion that, in turn, supports emotional regulation and complex problem solving. In Chapter 7, I discuss how to facilitate emotional regulation in students. Teachers pro-vide an emotional model for students. This model shows students how to feel good about themselves and how to cope with negative feelings.

The Co-construction of Narratives

The evolution of the human brain is interwoven with storytelling and the co-creation of stories among members of a tribe. A good story contains conflicts and resolutions, gestures and expressions, and thoughts flavored with emo-tion. Stories are then transferred from brain to brain across the social synapse and serve to integrate the functioning of individuals within groups by teaching skills, transmitting values, and creating shared perspectives and goals.

The coming together of these diverse functions sup-ports neural network integration. Teachers can employ narratives to reach students. Teachers can also help stu-dents rewrite their own narratives. This allows students to reframe past failures or traumas as growth opportunities.

No Clean Slates

Courage is acting in spite of fear.

Howard W. Hunter

The early years of life are a period of exuberant brain development that gives early experience a disproportionate impact on neural development. Thus, children enter school with brains already shaped by their families, neighborhoods, and cultures. A teacher can see a child's history reflected in his or her postures, attitudes, and words. By the end of the first day of class, teachers have a pretty good idea of the challenges that lie ahead. An early childhood that teaches children that the world is dangerous and that people are untrustworthy will not build a brain open to either teachers or new learning.

The fact that the brain is such a highly specialized social organ of adaptation is both good news and bad news. When good-enough parenting and other environmental factors combine with good-enough genetic programming, our brains are shaped in ways that benefit us throughout life. We are able to form meaningful relationships, deal with stress in a positive way, and be open to exploration and new learning.

The bad news? Our brains are just as capable of adapting to unhealthy environments and pathological caretakers. This adaptation may help us survive a traumatic household or neighborhood, but it may also impede our ability to connect with our teachers, learn in the classroom, or form trusting relationships throughout life.

On the other hand, we know that the brain is capable of change at any time and that social interactions are a primary trigger of neural plasticity. Close connections with teachers, friends, spouses—in fact, any meaningful relationship—can activate neuroplastic processes and change the structure of the brain, for better and for worse. Due to the interdependence of interpersonal experiences and biological growth, educators are particularly interested in the impact of significant attachment relationships on brain development.

We are social creatures with brains attuned to those around us. This means that we should seriously consider placing the same emphasis on social and emotional learning in the classroom as we do on memorizing facts and problem solving. Besides the obvious benefit of nurturing and raising better human beings, the attention to secure attachment relationships stimulates neuroplasticity and memory in ways that benefit all categories of learning and memory.

Reflection Box

Reflect for a moment about how much time and energy you invest in the content of your teaching versus your investment in your students as people living in the world. If your focus is almost exclusively on methods of distributing information, think of investing a bit more time in relationships in the months ahead and pay close attention to changes in classroom climate and student performance.

The vital implications for the classroom are: (1) place students and teachers at the center of the educational experience, (2) interweave the curriculum with team- and relationship-building exercises, and, where possible, (3) include a focus on self-awareness, compassion, and empathy into lesson plans. These changes will serve to activate primitive social instincts that will enhance all of our educational goals.

Creating a Tribal Classroom

Too few rejoice at a friend's good fortune.

Aeschylus

Unfortunately, creating a tribal classroom is a subversive act that is in opposition to the cultural obsessions of test scores and competition. It requires faith from the teachers, parents, administrators, and students that social and cognitive intelligence are of equal importance and that learning is best accomplished in the context of secure relationships. Ultimately, building a tribe is an art form guided by empathy, attunement, and human sensitivity. Thus, the tribal classroom needs to be firmly established in the hearts and minds of the teachers who will be the chiefs and of the parents and administrators who will support them.

While we wait for educational systems to wake up to the importance of attachment relationships to learning, teachers will need to be both clever and creative to build tribal classrooms. We have to figure out ways to embed tribe building into the curriculum, weave it into classroom management, and find time to dedicate to tribe building. Tribes can come in many shapes and sizes. What your particular tribe will look like will largely depend on your personality, interests, passions, and strengths. As the chief, your tribe will come to reflect who you are now and who you are capable of becoming with your students. It also depends on your particular school and the cultural, social, and economic factors surrounding you.

So how do you tap into these basic instincts in the classroom? Let's start with a basic definition: a tribe is a group of individuals tied together by time, familiarity, affection, and common purpose. While these four elements arise automatically in real tribes, they have to be created and nurtured in the modern world. A rule of thumb: whatever you can do to expand

and enhance these four factors, within the context of secure relationships, will support the creation of a tribal classroom.

Time

While you will naturally be spending time together in class, tribal classrooms are distinguished by time spent together that goes above and beyond the call of duty. This extra time, which you cultivate through socializing, field trips, or working on joint projects, appears important to distinguish a tribe from other classes. Another way to increase the subjective experience of time spent together is through increasing the emotional intensity of class time through experiences and exercises that are more personal and emotionally engaging.

Familiarity

Tribes are characterized by shared experiences, ongoing communication, and a lack of secrets. An important part of what is called team building in modern organizations occurred naturally during day-to-day life in tribes. Intimacy was created via continuous contact and knowing about each other's private lives as well as an emphasis on group identity.

Affection

Caring for others is grounded in compassion and empathy as well as in behaviors that demonstrate inclusion, democratic decision making, helping each other to accomplish goals, and sharing responsibility for success and failure. The value of everyone's experience is important to everyone; success is understood as a group goal rather than an individual accomplishment, and self-concept comes to include being a member of the group.

Common Purpose Through a Worthy Cause

For small-scale societies, the driving force behind the tribe is physical survival. I hope this is something you never experience in the classroom. What appears to activate the same emotions in students is group dedication to a worthy cause. In the process, cooperation and cohesiveness, trust and compassion are enhanced and expanded. The more important the task and the more difficult the challenge, the closer the bond—struggle, perseverance, and success cements group connection. The worthy cause can be directed toward a goal for the members of the class or a project that serves others. The important element is that the group sees it as both important and difficult to achieve.

Tribe building should be a specific focus early in the school year with considerable time dedicated to large-group, small-group, and dyadic interactions. The central goals of these interactions are personal sharing, building trust, and enhancing empathy. As the school year progresses, morning and afternoon times dedicated to these goals should become part of the schedule. The number of ways you can structure group interactions that support sharing and personal engagement are nearly infinite, and you should utilize those that you are most comfortable with.

The Goals of Tribe-Building Exercises

- Deeper knowledge of one another and an expanded sense of common humanity
- Deeper disclosure, sharing of emotions, and increased social support
- Having fun in learning while decreasing the stress involved in learning

The study of tribes and other kinds of groups can easily be connected to lessons related to culture, history, geography, language, ecology, social studies, and current events. Each of these lessons can then be tied back to the experiences of group process within the class. If you are fortunate enough to have a diverse group of students, you can assign a student to study the tribes of another student, interview the student and family, and learn about their history. This will also serve the goal of increased familiarity and affection. Exploring the family histories of each student can serve multiple functions—cultural education, self-disclosure, family involvement, and understanding the context for each student's view of the world and of themselves.

A good way to weave the establishment of a tribe into the curriculum is to study tribes from around the world. Discussions of the way small-scale societies make decisions, educate their children, and treat their elderly can all serve as guides to the establishment of class government, relationships, and sharing about the families and cultures each student comes from. You can talk about the social nature of the human brain by studying the power of ostracism in ancient Greece or the use of exile (such as Napoleon on Malta) to demonstrate the importance of relationships and proximity. You can even discuss the ethics of solitary confinement for prisoners. These lesson plans can help build the foundation for a tribal classroom.

There are countless books and websites where you can get ideas about specific group and tribe-building exercises, but no book can create the tribal center of gravity that needs to be established by the teacher in chief. In the same way, the flood of words and exercises that exist to promote social-emotional learning must be enlivened by emotion and not become robotic actions containing stale sentiments.

Exercise 2: Roadblocks to Learning

Reflecting on what we learned during the first assignment, we now explore the other side of the equation by asking these questions:

- What have been your most difficult learning experiences?
- When have you been unable to learn and why?
- What about other people makes it difficult or impossible to learn?

Repeat the same process of listening to everyone's stories and extracting principles that can be written on the board and sorted into categories. When this is complete, put the factors that enhance learning from the first assignment in a column on the left side of the board and those that inhibit learning on the right. Do your best to align them so that enhance and inhibit factors that relate to one another match up.

The next step is to explore the internal experience of how we feel in good and bad learning situations. Try to recognize when students are contributing thoughts instead of feelings and try to get them to the underlying feelings if they are having a difficult time. If a student says that someone looking over his shoulder makes him freeze up, you can ask him to try to identify what emotion is triggering the freeze (usually fear of failure).

It will become clear in the course of this discussion that the behaviors of those around us have a significant impact on our ability to learn. This is good evidence for the fact that the brain is a social organ and provides an experiential foundation for you to use the materials from this chapter to put together a basic lecture about the social brain. You may want to make copies of this chapter for high school students for reading and discussion. For younger grades, the principles of group dynamics may be best presented by using real examples from their experiences at school or in the community. The important piece is that students are able to appreciate and articulate the power of group dynamics on human experience and learning.

CHAPTER 3

Building Brains

Love is composed of a single soul inhabiting two bodies.

Aristotle

*F*or much of the twentieth century, there was a heated debate about the relative influence of genes and experience on brains, behavior, and human experience. The nature-nurture controversy was applied to everything from intelligence, to mental illness, to the ability to swim. In the past decade, this debate has been transformed into a deeper recognition of the profound interaction between genes and environment to a point where we now recognize that most human phenomena arise as an interaction between the two. The emergence of the field of epigenetics—the impact of experience on genetic expression—has provided us with a new framework to pursue the source of brain and behavior relationships.

Seven-year-old Trevor was brought to see me in my role as a therapist because his parents were concerned that something might be troubling him. He was very close to his grandfather, who had passed away six months earlier, but he didn't seem to have a reaction to this loss. While his parents felt they had done everything they could to encourage him to share his feelings, he didn't have that much to say. Trevor seemed to be a bright kid with interests in science, video games, and computers. As he became comfortable, we hung out, played, and talked about all kinds of things. During our second session, he mentioned that he liked doing puzzles.

Before our third session, I spread a puzzle out on the desk and put a few pieces together to give him a jump start. Trevor was excited when he noticed it and asked if he could help me work on it. "Certainly," I said, and we sat down to a session of puzzling. It didn't take long for me to realize that he was having difficulty, and I wondered if I had chosen a puzzle that was too difficult for him. The last thing I wanted to do was to give him a failure experience.

I suggested to Trevor that we didn't have to work on the puzzle if he would prefer to do something else. "Maybe this one is too hard for us," I said. "No," he replied with a smile, "don't give up. We'll get it." Impressed by his determination, we continued to move pieces around in search of colors and patterns. I became more and more amazed at his patience and dedication. Many boys his age would move on to something else or just clear the table with a swipe of an arm.

After a while, I heard Trevor mumbling under his breath. He was repeating something over and over like a mantra. I leaned over, slowly putting my ear closer and closer to him so that I could make out his words. Finally I could hear, "I think I can. I think I can." He was chanting the words from *The Little Engine That Could*. He was the little train that kept on keeping on. I immediately felt my eyes well up and had to resist the urge to hug him. Sure enough, he slowly got the hang of the puzzle and began to make progress.

I later found out from his parents that the *Little Engine* was his favorite story and one his grandfather loved to tell. It was clear that the Little Engine was a kind of hero to him. He used it when he was stressed by a challenging situation to soothe his anxiety and keep himself moving ahead. Part of this heroic story was likely the memory of a loving grandfather that he carried inside himself. Trevor was showing me the power of a story to soothe and inspire. I came to realize that his grandfather had done a wonderful job of becoming part of Trevor's inner experience. In many ways, he still had his grandfather with him. I believe that Trevor's ability to use narrative in this way and continue to feel his grandfather's love bode well for his healing. It warmed my heart to know that Trevor was the Little Engine who was brave enough to carry his grandfather over the next hill.

Brains were created to thrive on stimulation. In other words, they live to learn. This impulse is nurtured when it is rewarded by caring others. If a brain is unrewarded or punished for curiosity, it learns to hide, avoid risks, and stick with the familiar. While every child is capable of learning, some children have brains, minds, and hearts that have been turned off.

Fortunately, the brain is robust and wants to get turned on again. Relationships are usually the key to turning brains on. The difficulty in turning a brain on is often proportional to the experiences that shut it off. Kids like Trevor only need to be given permission to think in new ways and try new things; others need to be brought along gradually and given abundant support to cope with the anxiety triggered by new challenges. But how do teachers accomplish this seemingly miraculous task?

As social organs of adaptation, our brains continue to mature in a manner designed to meet changing social roles and expectations throughout life. This sustained plasticity serves the accumulation and transmission of nurturance and knowledge from one generation to the next. Trevor had a dedicated and loving grandfather who gave Trevor the inner strength and self-confidence to continue to explore the world without him—one amazing gift.

The Developing Brain

Nine-tenths of education is encouragement.

Anatole France

Some newborn animals can stand and walk on wobbly legs within a few minutes of birth. Soon after, they must follow their mothers to the next source of food or shelter. Unlike us, these animals rely on genetically preprogrammed wiring because they don't have the luxury of a gradual introduction to the world. From birth they have to be ready to contribute to their own survival by keeping up with the herd. Conversely, we humans are highly dependent newborns whose brains require decades to mature. This extended period of postnatal brain development makes ours among the most dependent and the most flexible brains on earth.

The brain is often talked about as having three layers, from bottom to top—the brain stem, limbic system, and the cortex. Although the brain stem is largely formed during gestation, the limbic system and cortex are shaped by experience as they adapt to our physical and social worlds. The cortex is very immature at birth, so infants rely on brain stem reflexes to organize much of their behavior. Brain stem reflexes orient the newborn to the mother's smell, to seek the nipple, gaze into her eyes, and grasp her hair. These and other reflexes jump-start the attachment process.

As the brain develops, neural networks from the cortex down to the brain stem inhibit reflexes and bring the body and emotions under increasing conscious control. Thus, a vital aspect of the development of the cortex is inhibitory—first of reflexes, later of spontaneous movements, and even later of emotions, impulses, and inappropriate behaviors. As we all know, the ability to inhibit motor movements, distraction, and emotions is what allows us to sit still, focus, and attend to classroom material. The difference between children's ability to do this reflects different levels of cortical development and maturity.

Neurons perform their complex symphony through a balance of *excitation* and *inhibition*. Just as it sounds, excitation activates neurons and inhibition shuts them down. When students are sitting quietly and attending to a lesson, they are engaged in a complex combination of selective excitation and inhibition that allows them to keep their bodies still while keeping their minds active. An active group project also needs a balance of excitation and inhibition but in a slightly different recipe.

It is within the matrix of family relationships that the networks dedicated to feelings of safety and danger, attachment, and the core sense of self are shaped. It may be precisely because there is so much neural growth and organization during *sensitive periods* that early interpersonal experiences are so influential. It was once thought that the brain didn't change much after childhood. However, we now know that there is considerable plasticity in the frontal lobes from the onset of puberty into our early twenties. It is now obvious to us that the upheavals of adolescence and early adulthood coincide with an exuberant period of brain plasticity.

Sensitive periods are times of rapid neural growth when specific skills and abilities develop. The timing of sensitive periods is genetically programmed and accounts for the rapid development of certain skills at approximate ages such as walking (twelve months) and talking (twenty-four months).

Consider the challenge faced by adolescents. For most of our evolutionary history, they have had to mature rapidly, form strong peer groups, and mate by their midteens. These challenges required a reshaping of attachment bonds from the values and structures of the family to peers and potential mates. They are driven by biological imperatives to establish an independent social identity, create new boundaries with their families, and find their own place in the world.

During adolescence, the brain is on its way to peak performance in areas of motor coordination, sensory refinement, and reaction time. Historically, these strengths in males contributed to the tribe's survival through improved hunting, foraging, and fighting. In females, increased focus on emotional connectivity, attachment, and interpersonal sensitivity prepared them for raising children and tribal bonding. When they are kept from their natural impulses and forced to engage in activities far afield from their innate drives, the teacher is in a position of trying to push a river upstream.

In most modern cultures, these real challenges are postponed for a decade or more. The postponement of the genetically timed challenges of mating, childbearing, and contributing to the tribe often leads adolescents to engage in nonproductive (and sometimes destructive) substitutes. I suspect that the mismatch between our primitive instincts and the structure of modern society leads to a great deal of the emotional distress adolescents carry into the classroom.

Teachers who want to capture the brains and minds of adolescent students should take these neural and historical factors seriously. Adolescents have been shaped by evolution to be engaged in important projects and intimate relationships, and to test the limits of their bodies and brains. All of us, especially adolescents, come to value the things and activities they invest in. If you can create a learning environment that calls upon them to take on serious challenges, most students respond. Get them out of their seats and out of the classroom as much as possible. Get them involved with important community projects where they can experience and respond to things that need to be changed in society. Convert their relationship with education from being passive recipients of information to active agents of change in their communities.

Application Box

Shape assignments to utilize these social energies in ways that contribute to society, broaden students' experience base, and test their skills of forming groups and achieving measurable results. Here is one example.

Assign groups of three to four students to research nonprofit organizations in your community for the purpose of having the class adopt their cause. Once the class decides on a specific organization, arrange a visit and look for opportunities for hands-on involvement. Consider creating a fundraising event that the students organize, market, and host.

Depending on the organization chosen, the problems it addresses can become part of the curriculum. Work at a homeless shelter could connect with lessons on the economy, racial discrimination, and mental illness. Raising money for cancer treatment could connect to lessons in biology, the way research is funded, or political issues of health care.

Adult students have different brains and other agendas. As we approach our thirties, changes in brain functioning reflect a move toward slower and more measured consideration; the brain adapts to new social roles that require deeper and more complex processing. The participation of multiple brain regions through adulthood allows for more inclusive and deeper consideration that serves increasing knowledge and problem-solving abilities, which are traditionally embodied in tribal elders. These are exactly the social and emotional skills required of teachers.

The co-evolution of the human brain with attachment, family, and culture strongly suggests that the life history of our brains is guided by our changing social roles. Declines in memory, attention, and the sharpness of our senses stand in stark contrast to improvements in systems dedicated to social judgment, expert knowledge, and emotional maturity. Although there may be a decreased need for new learning and quick reactions as we age, sustained attachment and emotional stability seem to be worthy of the body's continuing investment in social brain structures. Wise elders are essentially teachers who support the tribe through guidance, wisdom, and compassion, not a bad description for a teacher. Although teachers face many challenges, evolution and development have prepared us to guide our students.

How Experience Builds the Brain

The only way to control change is to accept it.

Chinese proverb

The science of biological inheritance began with Mendel's discovery of the basic principles of template genetics, or the way in which genes pass along traits from one generation to the next. We now know that while template genetics shapes the brain's infrastructure, neural networks are fine-tuned by experience through a process called transcription genetics. Therefore, when we connect to and teach our students, we are building the actual structure of their brains.

The term *epigenetics* is used to describe the guidance of genetic expression by experience via transcription. In other words, we all inherit a specific set of genes; which genes are expressed and which remain silent depends on experience. In effect, the strands of genes are like immensely long keyboards, and experience determines which notes are played. Experience can include anything from exposure to toxins and a high level of stress to a good education with a warm and loving teacher. As teachers, we attempt to use epigenetic processes to reshape the brains of our students to enhance their ability to think, learn, and act in more thoughtful and considerate ways.

Epigenetics is the study of how experience influences genetic expression during one's lifetime. The central epigenetic question for teachers is how we can shape the learning experience to optimize the impact on the structure and function of our students' brains.

The translation of experience into brain structure has broad implications for the transformative power of relationships and is particularly relevant for teachers. Teachers shape the brains of their students by the same epigenetic mechanisms as their parents. Many students spend more time in face-to-face interactions with their teachers than their parents, giving us plenty of opportunities to shape their brains. Let's take a closer look at these brain-shaping processes in action.

Research has discovered that maternal attention regulates gene expression in areas of the brain relevant to learning, stress regulation, and physical health. Increased maternal attention results in a variety of hormonal and neural processes that allow for the dampening of fear and anxiety and an increase in attention, curiosity, and exploration. See the box for some of the specific findings in each area of study.

The Impact of Nurturing and Attention

1. Improved learning via increased brain activity and neural growth
2. Greater coping skills in the face of anxiety, fear, and social-emotional challenges
3. Improved social connectivity, attachment, and bonding

Overall, animals who receive more maternal attention have brains that are more robust, resilient, and more inclined to nurture their own children. They learn more information, maintain memories longer, and are less reactive to stress. This array of factors is what you might expect to see in human children who are considered resilient and who are able to thrive in the face of physical and emotional challenges. This combination of positive attention and stress reduction has an extremely positive impact on classroom learning.

Less maternal attention has been found to correlate with fearfulness, anxiety, depression, and low self-esteem. Not surprisingly, low self-esteem is associated with higher levels of stress hormones as well as deficits in learning and short-term memory. Thus, it is clear that the way important adults treat children has been selected by evolution to shape their capacity to adapt and learn.

Fortunately, it has been found that positive social and physical environments can reverse the effects of early stress and deprivation. The fact that processes set in motion early in life can be modified by subsequent experience demonstrates the brain's ability to adapt to changing environments. On the other hand, chronic stress or trauma in adolescence and adulthood can reverse the effects of positive attachment earlier in life, reshaping the brain to resemble one that was deprived of early maternal attention. The implications of this research suggest that whatever differences children come to school with can be impacted by subsequent experiences in the classroom, especially teacher-student attachment relationships. Teachers can have a powerful influence on changing the brains of their students for the better.

Have you ever tried to learn to do something new with someone looking over your shoulder or with a critical onlooker? And what about the demoralizing and depressing effects that indifferent and disrespectful students have on teachers? Teachers depend upon a receptive audience to trigger their own positive biochemistry and brain growth. Teachers don't burn out from working hard; they burn out because they are frustrated, unappreciated, or hopeless about making a difference.

A caring, supportive other can create a state of body and mind that primes our brains to learn. We often find that high-risk children and adolescents who eventually have successful lives had one or two people who took a special interest in them—a mentor, teacher, or ballet or karate instructor—someone who knew them, gave them time, believed in them. This is not to be taken lightly; it points to the fact that we learn better when we are face-to-face and heart-to-heart with a significant other. A teacher's heart propels a student's mind. As Rita Pierson says, "every child deserves a champion."

Attachment and Bonding

The deepest principle in human nature is the craving to be appreciated.

William James

John Bowlby (1988) was a child psychiatrist who was especially interested in mother-child bonds, the importance of exploratory behavior, and the negative impact of separation and loss. His experiences led him to develop the concepts of *attachment figure, attachment schema, proximity seeking,* and a *secure base,* which are all relevant to a child's experiences in the classroom.

Bowlby's work, which highlighted the importance of specific caretakers to a child's sense of security, resulted in a major shift in the care of institutionalized children. To encourage bonding, children, who had previously been cared for by whoever was available, were now assigned consistent caretakers. In addition, this change in attitude transformed the role of nurses and caretakers from mere custodians to important attachment figures. It is clear that the same principles of attachment apply to teacher-student relationships throughout life.

An ***attachment figure*** is someone in a child's life who offers continuity and security, and who has the ability to soothe the child in times of stress. If a secure attachment is established, these early attachment figures become an unspoken template for what the child will seek out in others while becoming established in adolescent and adult relationships.

An ***attachment schema*** is the inner, unconscious representation of attachment figures that becomes activated in subsequent relationships, especially in stressful situations.

Proximity seeking refers to the tendency for everyone, but especially children, to move toward attachment figures when they are frightened, stressed, or uncertain.

Bowlby used the term ***secure base*** to refer to the attachment figure in a child's life to whom the child returns when he or she becomes frightened.

Although much of the attachment research has focused on the parent-child bond, the results are particularly relevant to teachers. Teachers follow parents as authority figures and as a central source of both nurturance and evaluation. Parents shape the attachment schemas that unconsciously guide their children's feelings, attitudes, and behaviors toward others, especially adults in positions of authority. Teachers further the shaping of attachment schemas through their interactions in and out of the classroom.

Bowlby suggested that early interactions create attachment schemas that he believed to be a summation of thousands of experiences with caretakers that become automatic, unconscious predictions of the behaviors of others. These schemas shape our first impressions, the kinds of people we are drawn to, and whether we feel relationships are worth having.

Attachment schemas are especially apparent under stress because of their central role in emotional regulation. They become activated when students are in a position of being judged by their teachers and peers. Thus, the establishment of secure attachment relationships soothes anxiety, allowing students to be more present and engaged with brains that are turned on to learning. Investing in building a tribal classroom goes a long way in building trust and enhancing security.

Reflection Box: What's My Attachment Style?

Take a moment to reflect on your own attachment style. Consider asking yourself the following questions. Do I sometimes rely on others for help or always try to be self-sufficient? What do I do when I'm feeling insecure in relationships? Withdraw, share my feelings, or do whatever I can to make the other person accept me? Do I have people who listen to and take care of me, or am I everyone else's caretaker? Reflecting on these patterns of behavior in relationships may give you some clues as to how you were shaped to relate to others, and it may be helpful in understanding how you connect with your students.

What Do I Do When I'm Afraid?

Do the thing you fear most and the death of fear is certain.

Mark Twain

Researchers study attachment schemas in one-year-olds in two stages. First, they are put under stress by being left alone with a stranger, and second, they are reunited with their mothers. How the child responds to the mother's return—the child's reunion behavior—is analyzed to determine the child's attachment style or schema.

Analysis of the children's reunion behavior has been organized into four categories: secure, avoidant, anxious-ambivalent, and disorganized. The general findings were as follows. Children who were rated as securely attached sought proximity with the mother upon her return; they were quickly soothed and quickly returned to exploration and play. These children seemed to expect that their mothers would be attentive, helpful, and encouraging of their continued independence. Securely attached children appear to have internalized their mothers as a source of comfort, which will often shape their relationships with their teachers and allow them to be more comfortable in a classroom setting.

Avoidant children tended to ignore their mothers when they returned to the room. They would glance over at her as she came in or avoid eye contact altogether. These children tended to have dismissive and rejecting mothers, and they appeared to lack an expectation that their mothers would be a source of soothing and safety. Children who were rated as anxious-ambivalent sought proximity, but they were difficult to soothe and slow to return to play. These children, who often had overinvolved or inconsistently available mothers, were slow to be soothed and tended to be clingy, and they engaged in less environmental exploration. These children will likely be less secure learners, and they may require more comfort and support to take risks in the classroom.

Finally, there was a group of children who engaged in odd behavior such as turning in circles or falling to the ground. They would freeze in place or have trancelike expressions. During later research, these children were included in a fourth category called disorganized attachment, and they often had mothers suffering from unresolved grief or trauma. Parents of children in this category demonstrated frightened and frightening behavior to their children. In school, these children may do everything possible to avoid attention, including behaviors such as keeping still and hiding in the back of the classroom. Alternately, they may exhibit odd and unpredictable behavior driven by their anxiety and fear. Both of these behaviors may alienate them from their peers, put them at risk for bullying, and impair learning.

Securely attached children do not produce adrenaline and stress hormones in response to stress, suggesting that secure attachment serves as a successful coping strategy. Those with insecure attachment schema do show a stress reaction. In other words, the behavior of insecurely attached individuals is an expression of arousal, anxiety, and fear. This knowledge may help us to be a bit more empathic for students who are, how shall we say, more difficult via inattention and disruptive behavior. Although these students are the most challenging, winning them over to learning is also one of the most rewarding aspects of teaching.

Application Box: Encouraging Contactful Anger

For those of us with insecure attachment styles, anger and disagreement are almost always experienced as cues for fear and abandonment. Yet it has been repeatedly shown that constructive disagreement and expressing negative feelings is essential to maintaining secure attachments and building functional work groups. Therefore, encouraging passionate yet respectful debate in the classroom will serve to enhance trust and build a more securely attached classroom. Some of the basic rules of debate such as turn taking, sticking to the issues, and avoiding personal attacks should be closely adhered to. It is also an excellent idea to have follow-up debates where students have to shift sides and argue against the position they were previously supporting.

Experiences of early disconnection and abandonment are at the heart of most human pain and can be the source of life-long feelings of brokenness. The possibility of healing this brokenness lies in being able to express negative feelings and have them be heard and accepted by caring others. Few children have someone with whom to discuss their fears and shame, so they grow into anxiety, self-doubt, and doomed attempts to be perfect. Creating the context for the expression of negative feelings and guiding the class to practice hearing and accepting is a priceless lesson in social-emotional development. Further, demonstrating that conflict can lead to resolution and reconnection are lessons that students will remember for a lifetime.

Every student enters the classroom with attachment schemas that impact their ability to connect with teachers and peers. An understanding of these schemas and what they reflect about a student's inner world can provide a great deal of valuable information for teachers. Regardless of the age of their students, teachers have the ability to stimulate neuroplastic processes and reshape brains in a positive, more adaptive direction. Secure attachment relationships are powerful tools in helping students to become competent and enthusiastic learners. See how these ideas are used in Exercise 3.

Exercise 3:
Caring for Ourselves
and Our Tribe

The assignment for this chapter focuses on bringing students' experiences at home and with their families into the classroom tribe. It serves two purposes; it expands an understanding of the social nature of the brain, and it brings students closer together by sharing their relationship histories outside of the classroom with their new tribe.

The central questions to explore are:

- What do I do when I'm stressed?
- What do I do when I'm sad?
- What do I do when I'm afraid?

Encourage students to give specific examples of the things that trigger these emotions and what they do to manage these difficult situations. The situations and coping reactions will differ across age groups, but the learning that will most often emerge will be related to the following questions:

- Do I move toward or away from others when I feel bad?
- Do others make me feel better, worse, or have no effect on my bad feelings?

- What are the spoken and unspoken rules in my family about how to deal with these emotions?

What will emerge are the coping strategies that students employ to regulate their negative emotions. The next question is whether or not the strategies they use and the rules in their families work for them. You don't have to (or want to) be too intrusive with these questions. Keep it light because these are difficult areas to explore—even a hint of disclosure about these issues will open someone's eyes to their own situation.

The final piece of this assignment is to open a discussion about how the new tribe that the class is creating together would like to deal with negative emotions. Some sample questions to open discussion would include these:

- Because negative feelings are inevitable, how should our tribe handle them?
- Should we set aside a special time to explore problems that come up (tribal council)?
- What is the best way for our teacher to handle negative feelings he or she is having?

The goal here is to normalize conflict and negative feelings and to establish a way for the tribe to process them. For many students, this may be their first experience with being invited to express negative emotions and having an agreed-upon way to deal with them. The overall goal of the assignment is to work toward a securely attached classroom tribe. Essentially, this means that when negative emotions are activated, individuals can come together and become reregulated through the support of the group and the help of the tribal leaders.

You may consider creating a rotating position of ombudsperson in the class. This person would be responsible for gathering information about a conflict and presenting it to the class. Training for this position would include listening and presentation skills as well as having an opportunity to present two sides of a case in an objective manner—very important skills for anyone.

It would also be a good idea to get advice from your school counselor about creating a protocol for how to deal with difficulties that may require a higher level of involvement by therapists or school administrators.

PART II

Turning Brains Off to Learning

CHAPTER 4

Stress and Learning: Vital Connections

Fortune favors the brave.

Virgil

A balance of challenge and support, stress and relaxation, and focus and fun are all aspects of successful teaching. In this chapter, we explore how the brain balances stress and learning via two structures, the hippocampus and amygdala. We also explore how the stress of learning can be counterbalanced by the timely use of humor.

For the most part, classroom learning and basic survival are worlds apart. But just below the surface, the biochemistry of learning and fear are deeply interwoven. When stress triggers bodily changes in preparation to fight or flee, energy is conserved by stopping the processes of growth—including the growth of the brain. When we are under stress, the body is pumped full of adrenaline and stress hormones, both of which interfere with learning. This is why learning gets turned off by anxiety, why stressed brains resist new information, and why fear and prejudice make us less intelligent. Understanding stress is central to successful teaching because stress disrupts every aspect of the attention, concentration, and memory required to learn.

Our experiences of anxiety and fear are the conscious emotional aspects of the brain and body's ongoing appraisal of threat. At its most adaptive, anxiety encourages us not to step off a curb without looking both ways and to check to see if we signed our tax forms before sealing the envelope. At its least adaptive, anxiety disrupts focused attention, halts exploration, and keeps us from taking appropriate risks. Anxiety can be triggered by countless conscious or unconscious cues and has the power to shape our behaviors, thoughts, and feelings. For those of us who tend to be anxious, our alarm system is like a smoke detector over the toaster. We get a lot of false alarms, and this makes it very difficult to learn.

Reflection Box

Think back to a time when you were really frightened. If the memory is still accessible, allow yourself to experience the changes in your body evoked by the memory. Now think back to thoughts or decisions made at the time. Can you identify any ways in which your perception or judgment may have been distorted or impaired by the situation? If so, consider how this level of fear or stress may have impacted your ability to learn.

As adults, we experience anxiety and agitation when we get criticized at work, engage in a heated debate, or get cut off on the highway. The same experience may be triggered in children and adolescents when they are called upon to speak in class, get bullied on the playground, or are faced with conflict at home. How others treat us has a direct and continuous impact on our ability to regulate our thoughts and feelings. Because of the interwoven nature of arousal, neural plasticity, and learning, the regulation of anxiety through secure attachment is one of the most powerful tools in a teacher's repertoire.

The Amygdala and the Hippocampus

Fear defeats more people than any one thing in the world.

Ralph Waldo Emerson

Although we tend to think of memory as a single function, we actually have a number of different memory systems. The two broadest categories of memory are conscious (*explicit*) and unconscious (*implicit*). When we design a classroom curriculum, we are primarily teaching information that will be stored in systems of explicit memory. However, sensory-motor, visceral, and emotional information is simultaneously stored in systems of unconscious, implicit memory. Explicit memory is organized by the coordination of the *hippocampus* in concert with multiple regions of the cortex. Implicit memory involves more subcortical and right hemisphere structures orchestrated by the *amygdala*.

> The *hippocampus* is a brain region specifically designed for the storage of short-term memory and the eventual transfer of this information to long-term memory. The hippocampus regulates *explicit memory*, which is another word for the brain's abilities to consciously learn new information. Activation of the hippocampus is modulated by arousal; it is particularly sensitive to high levels of stress.

The hippocampus is shaped like two seahorses toward the middle of the brain, one on either side. It is an essential structure for learning. The hippocampus also participates in our ability to use past memories and previous learning in new situations. The hippocampus and its connections with the cortex are noted for their slow maturation, which continues into early adulthood. They are also extremely sensitive to the negative effects of stress hormones (like cortisol) that inhibit brain functioning. Those of us who are chronically stressed have smaller hippocampi as well as deficits in short-term memory and learning.

The *amygdala* is a brain region that specializes in the rapid appraisal of experience as either positive or negative. When it detects something of interest, it triggers the hippocampus to start laying down memories. When it detects danger, it activates the fight-flight systems and inhibits new learning. The hippocampus regulates *implicit memory*, in which unconscious, traumatic, and early life experiences are stored. The emotions related to these memories get activated when we encounter danger signals.

The amygdala, our central hub for processing fear, is located beneath the cortex on each side of the brain. It functions as an organ of appraisal for danger, safety, and familiarity in approach-avoidance situations and plays a central role in social and emotional learning. As such, it is a key neural player in associating our awareness of potential danger with the activation of the fight-flight response.

In an unfortunate twist of evolutionary fate, the amygdala is mature a month before birth while the systems that regulate it take years to mature. Thus, even before birth, we are capable of being totally overwhelmed with fear with almost no ability to inhibit or regulate it. We are completely dependent on our caretakers to come to our rescue, and we use them to provide the self-soothing that we have yet to master. The way we are taken care of during childhood gradually shapes the neural circuits that we will eventually use to regulate our own emotions. And, although we have no conscious memories of our early interactions, these experiences greatly influence how we react in a classroom and throughout our lives.

The amygdala activates numerous targets in the brain stem, causing multiple physical expressions of anxiety and fear such as a racing heart, higher blood pressure, and fearful facial expressions. One job of the amygdala is to trigger the release of adrenaline in order to enhance vigilance and excitation while inhibiting activities such as paying attention to a lesson or learning new information. The relationship between the amygdala and hippocampus is extremely important to human learning. The balance between the two structures impacts emotional regulation, social relatedness, and our ability to succeed in the classroom.

In an optimal state, stressful experiences can be quickly resolved with good coping skills and the help of caring others. Sustained stress, on the other hand, results in a cascade of negative effects on the brain and the body. First, it inhibits protein production in order to maintain higher levels of metabolism. Because proteins are the building blocks of the immunological system, the suppression of protein production diminishes the body's ability to fight off infection and illness. Second, sustained higher levels of metabolism results in the death of neurons. Third, because the building of neurons depends upon the synthesis of protein, sustained levels of stress inhibit brain growth and learning.

If you are one of those people who believe that children are immune to stress, think again. Children who experience stress and trauma often perform far below their capabilities in situations requiring attention, concentration, and new learning. For these children, longer periods of relationship building and interventions focused on stress reduction and the development of coping skills are necessary prerequisites for success. Visiting children's homes and getting to know the social and physical environments they live in could go a long way in assessing their stress levels and the impact their environment has on their performance in the classroom. While we all know that it is impossible to eradicate stress, part of our job as teachers is to help our students regulate it and minimize its negative effects.

The Power of Mild States of Arousal

The oldest and strongest emotion of mankind is fear.

H. P. Lovecraft

The evolutionary logic of the link between learning and arousal probably goes something like this: when our needs for food, companionship, and safety are satisfied and nothing interesting is going on, there is no reason to invest energy in learning. At the other extreme, dangerous situations call for immediate action, and there is no time for new learning. In states of high and low arousal, cortical plasticity is shut down, and all available energy is diverted to survival and maintenance functions, respectively.

More than one hundred years ago, Robert Yerkes and John Dodson (1908) discovered a phenomenon that has come to be known as the inverted-U learning curve. The take-home message is that learning is optimized at mild levels of arousal and stress and turned off at moderate to high levels of stress. They charted their findings on a graph with arousal (or stress) on the x-axis, and performance (or learning) on the y-axis (see Figure 4.1).

Over the years, the same relationship was found to occur across species and in an array of learning tasks. Although this research took place long before anything was known about neuroplasticity, this inverted-U pattern has been found to parallel multiple aspects of the biochemistry of learning. At mild

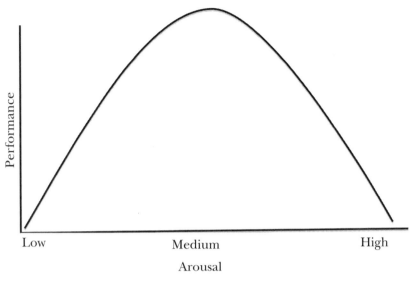

FIGURE 4.1 The Inverted-U Learning Curve

levels of arousal, the amygdala enhances learning by stimulating the release of low levels of *adrenalin* and *cortisol*. Through these chemical messages, the hippocampus is alerted to the importance of remembering what is being experienced. When we are too anxious or afraid, higher levels of adrenalin and cortisol inhibit learning.

Adrenaline is a hormone that is secreted when the amygdala detects danger to our physical or social survival. Adrenaline at high levels will lead to the inhibition of the hippocampus and learning.

Cortisol is a stress hormone that is secreted when the amygdala detects something of interest. At low levels, cortisol stimulates learning while at moderate to high levels, it inhibits learning. Sustained high levels of cortisol lead to shrinkage of the hippocampus and deficits in short-term memory and learning.

Learning's sweet spot occurs during a mild to moderate state of arousal (often described as curiosity or interest) that activates neuroplasticity and optimizes learning. Keeping students in the sweet spot of arousal is a core element in the art of teaching. We intuitively know that students need to have a bit of anxiety about grades to push them along but not so much that they are frozen with fear.

Teachers can use these principles to optimize neural plasticity in the service of learning. As we regulate stress in the classroom through our interpersonal skills and learning abilities, we are also manipulating the neuroplastic capabilities of the brains of our students. Tailoring tasks and feedback to match individual capabilities and emotional states are vital elements of this process. The safety of the emotional climate of the classroom is just as important. A student's openness to taking chances, exploring, and accepting new information are all indications that their curiosity is high and their anxiety is low.

Stress, depression, anxiety, and fear are all enemies of learning. They impair cortical processing and problem solving, and block the underlying biochemistry of neuroplasticity. This is why it is more difficult to learn or solve problems when we are anxious and depressed. One of the key values of secure attachment is the ability to soothe anxiety in the presence of stress. In secure attachment relationships, a child is able to use an adult as a safe haven and avoid experiencing autonomic activation in response to stress.

A secure classroom allows students to cope with the stress of new learning and regulate their fear of failure with the support of their teachers and fellow students. Whatever teachers can do to minimize anxiety and stress in their students and themselves enhances classroom learning. And because threats to our social and emotional well-being also activate the amygdala, attention to tribal solidarity is important for optimizing learning.

When I became anxious in school, I had difficulty understanding what was going on and struggled to pay attention. Eventually, I would just shut down, perform poorly on tests, and assume that I wasn't very smart. Having a way of talking about stress and a more objective perspective to explain it would have supported my learning while decreasing my sense of shame.

Consider making anxiety and fear a topic of discussion with your students, using the information from this chapter. Begin by having a conversation with your class about their personal experiences of anxiety and be sure to ask them if they ever feel like their brains are turned off when they are afraid. Consider teaching your students how to become anxiety whisperers.

Application Box: Becoming an Anxiety Whisperer

This process will take a number of hours and should be repeated and reinforced throughout the school year.

1. Draw the inverted-U curve on the blackboard and use whatever language you feel is appropriate to help students understand the relationships between anxiety and learning. Describe both ends of the curve and learning's sweet spot. Spend some time having students describe experiences of being enthusiastically absorbed in learning. You might describe it to them as interest, enthusiasm, absorption, or being caught up in learning.

2. Have each student draw his or her own inverted-U curve and write the numbers 1–10 along the arousal dimension (x-axis) from left to right. Next, label 1 as *drowsy* and 10 as *terrified* (or whatever words you feel would be better) and have them label numbers 2–9 with their own personal descriptions that go from words like *alert, interested,* or *enthusiastic* on the left to *overwhelmed, fright-*

ened, and *terrified* as they move to the extreme states on the right. Adjectives for the sweet spot may include *in the flow* and *firing on all cylinders* while nonoptimal states may include *checked out* and *at the beach.* Here is an example:

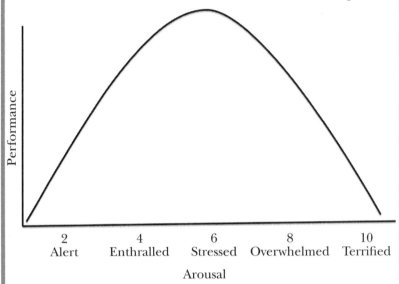

3. The next step is to have a class discussion about what they do to relax. This can include anything from yoga, to daydreaming, to doodling. Have students describe what they do to relax and what it feels like to relax. Be certain to compare it to anxiety and fear. Have the class explore techniques to relax that they can agree to try individually and together. The goals of this exercise are to come up with strategies that can be used in class to decrease anxiety. Have students vote on the variety of strategies that are described and discussed and pick one to use during class.

4. The final step is to practice having students monitor where they are on the inverted U and remember to engage in relaxation to bring them back into the sweet spot. The central lesson is that when they are on the right of the curve, very little learning will take place, so they need to

be aware of where they are, and getting back to the left side is essential.

Once this model gets established, you can reinforce this learning by randomly taking the class's anxiety pulse. Take a break from the lesson and ask everyone their number. If anyone is over 5, have the class take a 5-minute break to perform the agreed-upon relaxation exercise. Recheck everyone's number to see how effective it is and address the issues of any students who are still very anxious through a private meeting.

Although teachers need to learn to be anxiety whisperers, there are no standard formulas because brains, personalities, and learning styles vary. I'm sure that you have seen those who thrive at a specific level of stress while others crumble in the very same situation. Helping students to become anxiety whisperers will give them a tool that will be of help to them far beyond the classroom.

Humor in the Classroom

Man is the most intelligent of the animals, and the most silly.

Diogenes

A tried and true method of regulating anxiety and stress is through humor. This is why our everyday interactions are filled with smiles and laughter designed to decrease tension by communicating enjoyment and acceptance. Many studies have demonstrated what we already know—expressions of humor enhance feelings of intimacy and trust and make people more attractive and appealing. This may also be why "Makes me laugh" is such a common response (especially among females) to the question of what people find attractive in their partners.

It turns out that cracking or getting a joke results in widespread activation of frontal brain regions involved with emotional regulation, attachment, and the resolution of novel and incongruent information. To get a joke, we have to both appreciate the juxtaposition of unexpected information and get an emotional jolt from our reward system. This is probably why so much of our humor centers on the violation of expectations in social situations.

For example, John says, "My dad can beat up your dad!" Sam responds, "Oh yeah? How soon?"

The process of comparing expected with actual outcomes activates executive brain networks required for complex and abstract thinking. In fact, listening to humorous material has been shown to broaden the scope of attention and enhance performance on tests of creativity. Laughter obviously stimulates social connections and gets us emotionally in sync. Thus, humor serves the multiple functions of enhancing social connection, decreasing stress, stimulating brain growth, and enhancing neural network integration.

Application Box

Open Mike Afternoon: Except for school plays that usually involve a select group of especially talented and outgoing students, most students never get the opportunity to perform. What would it be like to have an hour each week set aside as performance time? Students could prepare 10-minute stand-up routines, karaoke performance, or group improvisation sketches.

Improvisations can be especially challenging and fun because the script is made up on the spot based on a suggestion from the class. For example, five classmates are told that they are marooned on an island and have to figure out how to be saved. Another group may be told that they have to figure out how to sneak a dozen mice though a security checkpoint in Mexico without being detected. The creative and fun things that come to mind under the stress of performing can create many laughs and good memories while supporting the development of cooperation and abstract abilities.

I believe fun presentation projects such as these are a good investment of time because they allow students to practice presentation skills, build self-esteem, and support the kind of tribal bonding we often see among the students that work together to put on plays. It would also be a good way to vent emotions, soothe stress, and weave humor into the classroom.

If humor can be used to stimulate neuroplasticity, activate executive brain regions, and enhance abstract processing, then it is a "no-brainer" that it can play an important role in the classroom. Using humor in the classroom has been found to increase students' attention, enjoyment, and memory. Researchers have found that when information is paired with humor, it is more likely to be rewarded, repeated, and remembered. Marketing experts, who have a huge stake in people remembering their messages, have also found that humorous advertising increases memory for products. The fact that it serves to bring people closer together and enhances participation supports its use as a vehicle of secure attachment.

When teachers use humor, it shows students that we are human, that we see them as human, and that we are making an emotional investment in the relationship. Not surprisingly, principals who share humor at school have teachers who report higher levels of job satisfaction. If you are still tempted to think that laughing and joking around is only a distraction in the classroom, take a look at some of the findings concerning the positive physical and emotional effects of humor and laughter.

The Benefits of Humor and Laughter

Intellectual
- Stimulates brain regions important for complex and abstract thinking
- Increases attention, improves memory recall, and increases conceptual understanding
- Activates brain growth hormones and associates classroom materials with pleasurable emotions

Emotional
- Provides a sense of empowerment and control
- Improves self-esteem, restores hope, and boosts energy
- Reduces anxiety, tension, depression, loneliness, and stress

Physical
- Improves respiration by exercising the lungs and chest muscles
- Improves mental functioning through increased neurotransmitter levels
- Decreases levels of stress hormones and strengthens immunological functioning
- Stimulates circulation (by increasing heart rate) and exercises and relaxes muscles

---

Laughter stimulates our brains to learn by increasing heart rate, depth of respiration, blood pressure, and activating muscles that secrete neural growth hormones. Higher levels of dopamine also reduce anxiety, fear, and sadness, while increasing energy, self-esteem, and a sense of empowerment. All of these changes signal the brain that it is time to pay attention and learn.

Caution: The effects of humor on learning depend upon a variety of factors, including whether the humor is expected, emotionally positive, and presented by the right people at the right time. In the classroom, derogatory humor and sarcasm, especially from the teacher, can impede learning. If humor is expected, it becomes a distraction and impairs recall, but it enhances learning when it appears at an unexpected time or in a surprising way.

As students spend more and more time being entertained by a variety of media, the challenge of capturing and holding their attention also increases. Since we can never be as exciting as video games or as tantalizing as Hollywood gossip, we have to capture our students' attention in other ways. I've found that even the most ardent gamer responds to warmth, humor, and a compelling story. It is no wonder that many highly successful educators blend stand-up comedy, drama, storytelling, and performance art into their teaching styles.

Based on all of these findings, you may want to enlist your class clown as a teaching assistant. He will get the attention he craves and the validation of being useful, and the other students may remember your lesson better. As Victor Hugo said, "Laughter is the sun that drives winter from the human face."

Exercise 4:
Learning to Chill

Teacher Self-Assessment

It is important to consider your own stress level, how you react to it, and how you react to your students' stress.

1. How can you tell when you are stressed?
   - What does this feel like?
   - How does it affect your teaching?
   - What do you do to cope with stress?

2. Now, think about the last time you were stressed in the classroom. What caused the stress?
   - Were there other factors that affected your stress level?
   - Could your students tell that you were stressed? How did they react?
   - How did you handle the situation?

3. How do your students exhibit stress?
   - How does this affect their ability to learn?
   - What do you currently do when your students are stressed? What techniques are the most helpful?
   - Do you utilize humor to reach your students during these times? If not, would you consider incorporating humor to reduce stress in your students?

- Based on the inverted-U learning curve, what are your current strategies for keeping students at optimal levels of stress?

Student Assessment

The central goals of this assignment are to (1) help students become more aware of their stress, (2) understand its negative impact on learning, and (3) become proactive in monitoring and regulating stress. The assignment starts off by having students think about the things that stress them out both in and out of school by asking these questions:

1.   Please write down three things that create stress in your life and rank them from the least to the most stressful. You will have a few minutes to think about this so you may want to write down as many items as you can think of and then pick the top three.

     As students share their lists, use the opportunity to point out the commonalities among them as a way to combat feelings of isolation or feeling weird. After about 5 minutes of open sharing, begin to focus on school-related stressors and write them on the board. Once this list is substantial, turn the group's attention to the next question.

2.   What impact does stress have on your ability to succeed in school? Think in terms of test taking, presenting reports, doing homework, and so on.

     Compile a list on the board of the ways that students experience stress and how it impacts their learning. Use this as an opportunity to share the inverted-U learning curve with them. This gives you an opportunity to teach your students a little neuroscience while providing them with a graphic representation of what is happening when their brains are under stress. Teaching them about the hippocampus, amygdala, adrenaline, and cortisol gives students a way to objectify what is happening inside them, and it provides a narrative that activates the cortical processing for them to better modulate their anxiety.

The third part is addressed in the form of a guided exercise. Turn the lights down and ask students to sit in their seats with their feet flat on the floor and hands in their laps. The instructions are simple.

3. Relax and pay attention to your breathing. If you notice thoughts arising, let them play out and move back to a state of thoughtless relaxation.

    Do this with the class for about 10 minutes (or shorter with younger children), and then have the class share their experiences. Ask some of these questions:

    •   Did any of you become relaxed? If so, what does it feel like to be relaxed?
    •   What challenges did you confront when you tried to relax?
    •   Was it hard or easy to keep your mind free from thoughts?

Becoming aware of the difference in mind and body between tense and relaxed states is an important first step in the self-regulation of stress. I would encourage you to make periods of meditation and reflection a part of your daily classroom routine and to encourage students to re-create a state of relaxed alertness when confronting those situations in and out of school that cause them stress. You can also incorporate these exercises before tests or other anxiety-producing activities.

Special note: If, in the course of sharing, a student shares a concern that is especially difficult, like a serious illness or death in the family, take the opportunity to abandon the assignment and focus on exploring the situation and supporting that stu-

dent if he or she appears to be open to it. Nothing supports
tribe building more than responding to personal crisis, while
nothing sabotages it more than a teacher who sticks to a plan
regardless of the human needs that arise. After dealing with
these situations in the best way you are able, you might consider sharing the experience with a school counselor in case a
student may need a referral for additional support.

CHAPTER 5

Reaching "Unteachable" Students

Character is fate.

Heraclitus

A central challenge to learning is shame. Shame comes in many forms but always feels the same—we feel worthless, unlovable, or just plain bad. It comes to those of all races, colors, and creeds and does not discriminate based on financial status or intelligence. When we focus on teaching information while neglecting shame, we run the risk of completely missing our students. In the following pages, we explore the origins and expressions of shame, how it appears in the classroom, and how we can combat its negative effects.

There is an intimate connection between social acceptance and learning. Have you ever felt smarter and more articulate with a receptive and enthusiastic listener? How about when you are speaking to an audience that is obviously bored or critical? In these situations, we can almost feel our IQ melting away.

When I was in college, I had a particularly memorable encounter with a very good listener. A friend had asked me for a ride to a retreat center where he had an appointment to speak with a teacher to get help with a paper. We arrived at a beautiful wooded setting, and I excused myself to take a walk around the grounds.

After walking along wooded paths for a few minutes, I came upon a bench next to a lake and sat down. A minute or two later, a man walked up, said hello, and sat down. His approach was so natural and relaxed that I first assumed he had mistaken me for a friend. He introduced himself as Jon, told me that he was staying at the retreat to work on a paper, and immediately began asking me questions. He wanted to know about my studies and the ideas that I found most exciting. He asked with such sincere interest and enthusiasm that he seemed to find ideas in me that I didn't know I had. I felt stimulated by our connection and could feel that I was pushing the envelope of my thinking.

Time flew by as we bantered back and forth. Eventually, we were interrupted by calls from my friend. Regretfully, I bid Jon goodbye with a promise to return to renew our discussion. As my friend and I drove back to campus, I noticed a brochure from the retreat facility in the car. As I unfolded it, I saw a picture of Jon with the caption "Dr. Jonas Salk." I was stunned and temporarily speechless. Eventually, I told my friend that this was the man I had been talking to for the last hour. My heart pounded as I began to think of all the foolish things I had just said to the man who cured polio.

Had I known I was talking to Jonas Salk, I would have been overwhelmed with anxiety, self-doubt, and shame. If I were able to speak at all, I probably would have been all jumbled in my thinking or, even worse, I would have tried to sound smart. Instead, my lack of self-consciousness combined with his sincere interest raised my game in a way that I will never forget. I now realize that his curiosity, enthusiasm, and openness stimulated my brain to work better. A good listener, combined with the absence of shame, provides an optimal neurobiological environment for creativity and learning.

The other lesson I took from this experience was the power that Dr. Salk had to make me feel important and intelligent while inspiring me to new levels of expression. Although we think of intelligence as something that resides in our heads, the ability of one person to stimulate thinking in another suggests that intelligence is a collective process. We are far smarter when linked to those who accept, respect, and encourage us. We can create similar settings in our classrooms by becoming compassionate and skilled listeners.

Although encouraged by society to be strong and independent, most of us enter adulthood with insecurities about our value, worth, and lovability. To protect ourselves against these painful feelings, we build defenses that keep our vulnerabilities at bay. My pain in not feeling valued by my father during childhood affected almost all of my relationships with adult men, especially those in authority. What most impressed me during my brief encounter with Dr. Salk was my sense of safety and lack of defensiveness. His interest, vulnerability, and openness were true gifts.

The Burdens of Childhood

What do you regard as most humane? To spare someone shame.
Frederick Nietzsche

Scanning the faces of new students each fall, we see in their expressions a reflection of the ways in which their brains have been shaped to cope with the world. Some are empty vessels eager for new learning, others are terrified, still others are too numb to learn. One girl may seem off in another world, while the boy next to her is teasing the boy next to him, trying to provoke a fight. The girl next to them may be struggling to pay attention through all of the distractions. Some students are struggling to build their sense of self-worth while others are already convinced they are worthless. Creating an optimal learning environment requires the ability to uncover and heal old wounds that interfered with learning.

Children are born with millions of years of animalistic instincts; they want to be the center of attention, win all the prizes, and be adored for everything they do. They want to fly like a superhero, be the most popular kid on the playground, and never have to wait their turn. On the other hand, most parents want a child to be respectful, hardworking, and well behaved. Gradually shaping children's primitive self-centered instincts into healthy and realistic self-esteem without crushing their spirit is central to both parenting and teaching.

This sort of socialization involves lots of no's, don'ts, disappointments, power struggles, and time-outs. Most children aren't harmed in this process; part of life is absorbing plenty of negative feedback. Problems in psychological and intellectual development occur when the normal egocentrism of childhood is met with prolonged and overwhelming experiences of criticism and rejection. This can occur due to harsh parenting or an oversensitive temperament that overwhelms a child's ability to cope with anxieties and fears.

To begin understanding the power of *core shame*, we first need to distinguish it from appropriate shame based on selfish or thoughtless behavior. It is appropriate and important for us to experience shame when we have violated the values of our group and have treated others badly. This sort of shame, the kind that gets people to say "Shame on you!" supports social learning and the development of empathy.

Core shame is the experience of being flawed and unlovable, which is completely disconnected from our actual behavior. It is as if we have been tried and convicted of some crime that we don't remember committing. Core

> shame leads to perfectionism, rigidity, and anxiety—all of
> which impede creativity, exploration, and learning.

The term core shame is reserved to describe the experience of being fundamentally defective, worthless, and unlovable as a human being. Core shame (the opposite of self-esteem) creates unteachable students via a spectrum of defensive thoughts, feelings, and behaviors designed to protect them from pain—especially new authority figures in a position to judge them.

To be successful with shame-based students, there is damage to undo before learning can take place. Once core shame is addressed, students are better able to learn, grow, and explore. In fact, the most important gift any teacher can give to children is to help them transcend shame to a place of curiosity, exploration, and the joy of discovery. The vehicles for this transformation are dedication, compassion, and love.

Reaching the "Unteachable"

I learned that courage was not the absence of fear, but the triumph over it.

                                        Nelson Mandela

I've heard the label "unteachable" used twice: once to describe children with severe brain damage and once to describe underprivileged minority students in inner-city schools. I feel that to whatever degree students with intact brains are *unteachable*, it is not because they lack the capacity to learn. Rather, they lack the social skills, emotional resources, and behavioral abilities to sit still, attend, and learn in a typical classroom. Neuroscience is revealing the brain to be quite resilient and capable of reversing the effects of early negative experiences. We can see this in action through the work of Marva Collins (1992).

Through attachment-based teaching, Collins has been success-ful with many children previously considered unteachable. Her target was the core shame her students brought into class with them from their experiences in family, community, and institutionalized prejudice.

> Children and adolescents can come to be labeled as **unteachable students** if their brains have been turned off to learning in a classroom setting. The array of causes for this state of mind, brain, and body include neglect, abuse, and cultural prejudice. It is also caused by a mismatch between students' interests, abilities, and needs as well as the educational context in which they are being so labeled. This unteachability isn't an aspect of the student's brain, but an unfortunate person-environment interaction.

As a public school teacher, Marva Collins came to believe that students could not succeed in a system where prejudice and failure were the norm and where no attention was paid to the emotional well-being of students. She realized that reach-ing and teaching at-risk students would take a caring and sup-portive environment that resembled a nurturing family. When she could no longer stand to watch what she called the institu-tionalization of failure, she took $5,000 from her pension fund and opened Westside Preparatory School on the top floor of her Chicago brownstone. Her mission was to teach failures, dropouts, and those deemed unteachable by the system.

Ms. Collins welcomed each new student with an assault on shame: "Welcome to success and say goodbye to failure because you are not going to fail. I'm not going to let you fail. You are here to win, you were born to win, and if I have to care more about you than you care about you, then that's the way it will be" (1992, p. 16). By taking this firm and loving stance, she made herself emotionally available while establishing the expectations and values of her new tribe.

Her message was simple—there are no miracles in successful education; it just requires endless commitment and determination grounded in love and security. She recognized the devastating effects of failure, rejection, and shame in the faces of her students, and she met them with total dedication and love. Her philosophy of education is grounded in humanity, compassion, and an appreciation of the total child—a philosophy similar to tribal cultures that consider children as gifts from god.

While most teachers focus on the bright students sitting at the front of the class, Collins looks for the "dirty little ones" who sit in the back of the class or who stand by themselves on the playground. These are the children who are neglected or abused at home, who don't get warm meals, and who haven't learned to care enough about themselves to learn. She advises teachers to go to the back of the room and find ways to connect those students with the others. She encourages teachers to say something positive about each student every day.

She feels it is her responsibility to let her lesson go for a few minutes to find out what is bothering a child. Her method is to first make an emotional connection with the child, and then they make a commitment to solve the problem together. She believes that teachers should never say anything negative about their students, that they should be showered with compliments and encouragement, and that it takes more courage to take a chance and be wrong than to play it safe and not try.

Collins tells a story of a student who had never done well in school, seemed completely unmotivated, and had given up on himself. Day after day, she would sit down next to him, do his work for him, and give him A's. He was shocked and thought she was crazy. His mother even complained to Collins that something must be wrong with the school if her son was getting A's. Her strategy was to get him accustomed to receiving A's, learn to be a proud student, and then let his pride and self-esteem support his learning. He increasingly participated in his assignments and eventually mastered them.

Instead of consequences and punishment, Collins's discipline comes in the form of loving lessons designed to teach and reconnect with her students. She said, "When you must reprimand a child, you do so in a loving manner. Don't ever try to degrade or humiliate him. His ego is a precious thing worth preserving. Try saying: I love you very much but I will not have that kind of behavior" (1992, p. 196). She nurtured her emotionally wounded children back to intellectual health by caring for them as if they were her own, saying, "great teachers don't send bad kids to the principal's office. They go up to the child, hug them, and tell [them] that they care" (p. 36).

She argues that when children feel good about themselves, they have no reason to act out. Acting out is a sign that something is wrong within a child who lacks the ability to articulate his or her feelings. If these children are left on their own and then get into trouble, it is far more difficult to reach them if you haven't already established a connection. When children feel unloved and abandoned, they feel empty, and their emptiness fills with pain, rage, and violence. Collins's experiences have taught her that loving her students lessens the fear that drives their rebellion.

> **Reflection Box**
>
> Think for a moment about how you might be able to incorporate Collins's methods into your teaching style. Do you remind yourself to stay positive or to take a moment to express your gratitude to your students? Do you try to begin every interaction with a compliment? Before you provide constructive criticism, are you sure to identify the problem behavior as separate from the student? Do you remember to add, "I know that you can do better in the future"?

The Teacher as a Safe Haven and Holding Environment

Tolerance is the best religion.

Victor Hugo

Marva Collins is a matriarchal elder who addressed the central issues of shame, self-esteem, and compassion by creating a tribal environment and safe haven for students who could not succeed in large public schools. She would tell a child, "Look, I love you but you have to get your act together. You're going to learn or you're going to die." This is the message of the tribe—learning is not optional; it is necessary for our survival. We are all depending on you, and you must take responsibility for your life and the lives of those around you.

Collins said to think of classes as loving families that create a climate of care and support. She encourages us to have physical contact with students, to take a student's hand, or to give one a hug. She reaches out, touches a student's face, lift his chin, and says, "Speak up honey, you're brilliant." She believes that creating an exciting, stimulating, and emotionally safe classroom is the best way to gain and maintain attention. Perhaps her most important lesson is that teachers should always be actively rooting for their children to succeed.

In his writings, John Bowlby (1988) emphasized the importance of a *holding environment* created by a safe haven. A holding environment is a relationship that is safe enough to allow for fear, confusion, and uncertainty while supportive and encouraging of growth. The security that is established within a safe haven allows for a suspension of self-defense, which frees up the energy and focus needed to revisit and heal emotional wounds. This is what needs to occur in good parenting, teaching, and other forms of mentorship.

A **holding environment** is an interpersonal space that creates emotional regulation, safety, and encouragement in such a way that it supports mutual trust, exploration, and adaptive learning.

In the midst of all of her attention to the social and emotional elements of a successful classroom, Collins also emphasizes high standards and hard work. She feels that lowering standards and allowing kids to slide only reinforces their lack of self-worth. She states, "Mediocrity, complacency, and a general lowering of standards are and have always been the antagonists of freedom in the saga of human life" (1992, p. 53). She teaches us that love, affection, and high standards can go hand in hand. How do you feel about this?

From Whence So Much Shame?

There is no witness so terrible and no accuser so powerful as conscience which dwells within us.

Sophocles

During the first year of life, parent-child interactions are mainly positive, affectionate, and playful. Infants' limited mobility and skills keep them close to caretakers who provide for their physical and emotional needs. As infants grow into toddlers, their increasing motor abilities, impulsivity, and exploratory urges lead them to plunge headfirst into danger. The unconditional affection of the first year gives way to loud and abrupt inhibitions designed to stop children in their tracks. A chorus of loud "no's" replaces the smiles and soft tones. A shift in the use of the child's name from a term of endearment to a warning is familiar to us all.

This warning mechanism, seen in many social species, is designed to make children freeze in their tracks in order to protect them from predators and other dangers. Experientially, children are snapped from a mode of curiosity, exploration, and excitement to one of fear, hypervigilance, and withdrawal. The same response is seen when a dog hunches over, pulls his tail between his legs, and slinks away after being scolded for some canine faux pas. Similar postures occur in reaction to social exclusion, helplessness, and submission in virtually all social animals. It is nature's way of expressing, "You are the alpha and I'm not—please don't hurt me." But for young children, these same interactions mean, "I'm not important, valuable, or lovable enough to be a valued member of the family"—an experience that feels life threatening when your survival depends upon your family's protection.

These experiences may occur in early attachment relationships when an excited expectation of connection in a child is met with indifference, disapproval, or anger from a parent. It has been hypothesized that experiences of disconnection trigger the same rapid shift from excitement to withdrawal. While it may be difficult for adults to remember, toddlers expect their parents to be just as curious and excited as they are about covering the floor with milk or flushing the phone down the toilet. Also, because core shame is formed during a developmental period characterized by an egocentric perspective, we believe that parents don't leave a marriage or die from an illness; they abandon us because we were not lovable enough for them to stay.

Disruptions of attunement and emotional connection can happen between the best of parents and the healthiest of children. However, a child with a sensitive or anxious temperament may suffer greatly in the face of what appears to be normal, everyday parenting interactions. These children will also be strongly affected by criticism in the classroom. In other families, parents who were abandoned, neglected, or abused as children may use criticism as the predominant parenting style with their own children. This is quite common in rigid and controlling parents, religious cults, and military families, or when there is mental illness in one or both parents. Teachers raised this way may also be vulnerable to using shame as a method of controlling their students.

Reflection Box

Take a few moments to reflect on some of the things that made you feel insecure and ashamed as a child. Think about ways in which it is difficult to accept yourself today. Seeing through our own defenses and allowing ourselves to feel vulnerable are powerful bridges for empathy with our students.

For social animals like ourselves, the fundamental question "Am I safe?" has become woven together with the answer to the question, "Am I lovable?" Core shame results in a sense of being flawed and defective, which results in a preoccupation with being found out. The fear of being exposed as a fraud drives a relentless and fruitless battle to be perfect, which results in alternating anger and exhaustion. Although people with core shame cannot figure out what they have done wrong, there is nothing they can do to redeem themselves (Brown, 2012; Kaufman, 1974). Children riddled with core shame enter the classroom anxious and fearful, anticipating criticism and eventual exclusion. This makes it difficult for them to be vulnerable enough to even attempt to learn.

The Stage and the Classroom

Criticism comes easier than craftsmanship.

Zeuxis

Our fundamental sense of self-esteem and shame are programmed in the first few years of life. Because they are forms of preverbal learning, they are deeply known but never directly thought about. By the time we achieve self-awareness between five and ten years of age, positive self-esteem or core shame are already social and emotional givens. Similar in many ways to turning on your computer and viewing your screen, you accept the reality of your workspace unaware of the thousands of lines of programming language that created it.

As you might imagine, core shame is usually an aspect of the lives of both bullies and their victims. Shame becomes especially prominent during adolescence due to the heightened emphasis on being cool, acceptance into new groups, and dating. Core shame distorts social cognition and creates the experience of rejection in neutral and even positive situations.

Consistent misperception of rejection and negative distortion of social interactions create a vicious cycle that aversively impacts popularity, social status, and the ability to form relationships. In this way, core shame becomes a self-fulfilling prophecy—an expectation that we turn into a reality.

For those with core shame, even relatively minor abandonment is experienced as life threatening because it triggers implicit memories of shame. Any feedback suggesting less than perfect performance triggers panic, making it difficult to take risks or explore new ideas. In some adults, core shame is acted out by choosing abusive or nonsupportive partners, perfectionism, and a lack of self-care.

You see expressions of shame in an inability to tolerate being alone or in adolescents and adults who attempt suicide after a breakup. In their behavior with others, they are characterized as compulsive apologizers, desperately trying to avoid conflict and the anger of others, which always feels deserved. Praise bounces off them, but anything with even a hint of criticism will be taken hard and never forgotten. In the classroom, this puts teachers in a precarious situation because our words have the power to do both great good and great harm.

Because uncertainty is intolerable, students with core shame have great difficulty when they do not know an answer. These students, who may be quite intelligent, won't try anything unless they feel certain of success. This also keeps them from being open to new material, taking on challenges, and learning how to regulate feelings of insecurity on the way to mastery. See Table 5.1 for some of the correlates and consequences of core shame.

One of my students described it this way: "My shame makes it impossible for me to be loved because I can never believe someone could love me. And if they do, I can't possibly respect them because their judgment must be seriously flawed." Because shame shuts our brains down to new learning, establishing

TABLE 5.1 The Consequences of Core Shame

School Performance	Biological
Fear of negative evaluation	Decreased immunological
Increased shame in the face	functioning
of failure	Increased levels of cortisol
Maladaptive perfectionism	Decreased neuroplasticity and
Inability to risk making a mistake	learning
Reduced pride in response	
to success	

Social	Emotional and Psychological
Conflict avoidance	Depression
Anger, hostility, and	Inferiority, low self-esteem, and
externalizing problems	low self-efficacy
Envy and blame of others	Inappropriate self-blame
	Reflective apologizing
	Reduced interpersonal
	problem solving

nonshaming relationships with these students is a necessary prerequisite to successful teaching. But as you can imagine, they are going to test you and make you prove you are worthy of their trust; they have been betrayed before.

Those who suffer from core shame often describe early parental relationships as having included abuse, abandonment, and criticism. Others describe dependent parents who, instead of helping them develop, looked to them for care and emotional support. In both cases, the absence of caring and competent parenting makes children extremely vulnerable to core shame. This is another reason why it is so helpful to interact with parents. Although you may not be able to improve the situation at home, you can adjust your techniques in the classroom to adapt to a child's emotional needs.

In the classroom, shame-based students struggle to be perfect while living in fear of the teacher's constructive criticism. Some develop an overwhelming fear of being laughed at or of blushing, which keeps them from raising their hand and speaking up in class. While the physiology, emotional expressions, and triggers for shame have cross-cultural commonalities, variations emerge from different histories, morals, and customs. Because of this, it is important to learn about (and be sensitive to) what it means to have pride and to keep "face" in someone's culture, subculture, or gang. In general, the more disrespect a group has had to endure, the more important being respected is for its members.

Application Box

The topic of respect will stimulate class discussion and is an excellent way for everyone to get to know themselves and each other a little better. You can start off the discussion by exploring various definitions of respect and the social and emotional experience of saving face. You might even start by sharing some personal examples of your own thoughts about and experiences of shame. With older students, these concepts can be examined across contexts (friends, family, school, and so on) and across cultures. These discussions can provide you with a window to the inner worlds of your students.

Children with parents who have problems with addictions or the law may have their core shame compounded by conscious embarrassment about their family members. Often, children are more deeply connected to parents who mistreat them, so don't assume that abused and abandoned children don't blame themselves for what has been done to them. As a result, a kind and attentive teacher may be attacked by a neglected student because being cared for activates pain about the parents he or she never had. Until a teacher is able to overcome this reaction, none of your good deeds will go unpunished. It takes time for students to adjust. Be patient.

We also need to remember that teachers can be as vulnerable to shame as their students. Have you noticed how good kids are at detecting and exploiting your weaknesses and insecurities? Your unexplored shame, fears, and vulnerabilities may become an Achilles' heel, making it difficult to establish and maintain the posture of wise elder with a challenging class. Just as in students, teachers' emotional maturity and self-knowledge can make all the difference in their success. Be sure to invest the time to explore, understand, and heal some of your own brokenness before you take charge of a classroom.

Radical Acceptance

Don't turn away. Keep your gaze on the bandaged place. That's where the light enters you.

Rumi

Because we are social creatures, loving relationships are as important to our growth, health, and learning as nutrition, exercise, and sleep. Through attachment and compassion, teachers can create a tribal classroom that supports inclusion, acceptance, and security. Brain systems responsible for attachment remain flexible (plastic) throughout life and the teacher has the power to influence and alter earlier negative attachment experiences.

We know that social interactions early in life result in the stimulation of both neurotransmitters and neural growth hormones that participate in the active building of the brain. By re-creating a positive parenting relationship, it is highly likely that empathic connectedness stimulates biochemical changes in the brain capable of enhancing new learning.

It does take a village to raise a child, and a teacher can create a tribal village in the classroom. Tapping into the power of our primitive social instincts and activating plasticity in attachment circuitry can gradually counteract many of the negative effects of core shame. Along the way, teachers are activating many of the same biological and neuroanatomical changes that occur during parenting. Because of this, "in loco parentis" (in place of a parent) is more than a legal term related to custodial responsibility; it also reflects teachers' power to influence their students' brains. Tribal teachers become loving and protective parents to their students, who in turn can become caring and supportive siblings to one another.

The teacher is capable of becoming the student's secure base by expressing caring concern, a willingness to listen, and proving that he or she can be trusted. This secure attachment allows students to use teachers to help regulate their anxiety in the face of new challenges. This emotional regulation, in turn, allows neural networks dedicated to new learning to stay active and engaged, and grow. Being prepared to recognize and greet each student by name on the first day of school will be the best prep time ever spent. I bet they will remember the positive surprise of being known far longer than the information you will communicate during the year.

Contrary to the assembly-line mentality of education, sustained secure attachments provide a positive and cost-effective way of improving the performance of all students, especially those traditionally considered to be at risk for failure. We all need to find a way to make the establishment and maintenance of secure attachment a central focus in learning and education.

Exercise 5: Understanding and Combating Shame

Understanding Shame

The goal of this exercise is to gain a deeper understanding of how shame affects our lives and how to combat it.

Shame is part of being human and although most everyone experiences shame, it makes some individuals feel cut off from others and very alone. Talking about it can be difficult, and it is extremely helpful if a teacher is able to talk about those things that cause him or her shame. This exercise consists of four steps: (1) defining and describing shame, (2) having students share their own experiences of shame, (3) understanding how hurtful and damaging it can be for self-esteem and learning, and (4) making a commitment to try to limit self-shaming and shaming interactions with others. Because shame is at the core of most of our suffering, this exercise may go on for many sessions. It is likely that it will bring up difficult emotions, so be prepared to stop the exercise to attend to individuals who need support. Don't be attached to completing the exercise—attend to whatever significant material emerges.

As the first step, use the information in this chapter to define, describe, and differentiate among guilt, healthy shame, and core shame. Present a minilecture pitched to the age and sophistication of the group rich with examples of what it would look and feel like for them. What you want to focus on here is the fear of being unloved by parents and peers. Adolescents are consumed with being accepted, attractive, and cool. For younger children it may be reflected mostly in a fear of being laughed at for doing something poorly and an avoidance of taking risks when they are uncertain of their abilities.

The second step is to ask each student to describe or write down a few examples of things they are ashamed of and see if they are experiences of guilt, healthy shame, or core shame.

- What does it mean to fail, make a mistake, or be imperfect?
- What does it mean to not be the most popular girl or the most athletic boy?
- What does it mean to get a B instead of an A?

For other kids who are not connected to academic success, the discussion should be directed toward success in whatever area they find value, such as family acceptance, performance in sports, or popularity with their peers.

We compare our insides to everyone else's outside and feel lacking.

How do you defend against your shame?

- Perfectionism: If I do everything perfectly, no one will know that I am a fraud.
- Arrogance: It's hard to be surrounded by such losers.
- Exhibitionism: Look at how great I am!
- Withdrawal: I know I'm not good enough so I won't be part of the group.
- Denial: I am not ashamed of anything.

Combating Shame

Ways to Combat Shame

Learn about the negative impact your shaming has on others and yourself.

Make a contract to stop shaming others directly in your behavior toward them or through gossip behind their backs. The greatest reward for not shaming is an increase in respect for yourself.

Learn to connect the way you shame others and the shame you feel within yourself. This form of projecting is doing unto others what others (and now you) do to you.

Reality Testing

We often fear that we have negative qualities that are obvious to everyone around us. One way to reality test this is to share fears about yourself with others and ask for feedback in what could be called a 360-degree evaluation from your peers. Another way to reality test is through logic—for example, people who feel like they don't have friends could think of who they could call if they needed someone to talk to or help with their homework.

I'm Not Perfect but I'm Good Enough

What does it mean to accept our basic imperfections and to learn to be at peace with being good enough? This includes a discussion about perfection as an abstract and unattainable goal and what the true human condition looks like.

What Do I Have Going for Me?

Most of us are punished for bragging. The unfortunate thing is that many of us come to only focus on our weaknesses and forget our strengths. Writing a brief biography and making a list of strengths is something that can rebalance this and something we can use in times of distress.

See Potter-Efron and Potter-Efron (1989) for more details and practical exercises.

CHAPTER 6

From Bullying to Burnout: How Social Stress Undermines Students and Teachers

What wisdom can you find that is greater than kindness?

Jean-Jacques Rousseau

Acceptance and appreciation are fundamental human needs. This is why losing face, being shamed, or being sent into exile result in emotional and even physical pain. While students are striving to develop an identity, find a place in the social order, and establish safe and secure relationships, teachers are doing the same with colleagues, administrators, and in their personal lives. We all strive to be accepted, respected, and valued by members of our tribe. In this chapter we explore this human struggle and the consequences of bullying and burnout in our classrooms.

Before I trained to be a psychologist and teacher, there was a period of time when I had two half-time jobs. Each morning, I made sandwiches behind a deli counter, after which I drove across town to load trucks in a warehouse. At first it seemed like a good balance, and I was especially thankful for the hard physical labor given my lack of willpower in the face of so much pastrami and chocolate cake. The most amazing, confusing, and painful aspect of this time in my life, and the reason I'm sharing the story, was the stark contrast between how I felt at each of the jobs.

When I arrived at the deli near sunrise, the crew had already been there for hours preparing food for the day. They were joking, telling stories, and happy to have me join in the mix. The first sleepy customers were greeted with smiles and fresh coffee, with all but the grumpiest responding with a smile. The boss liked my work and expressed interest in my personal life and future career plans. Despite the difficult hours and the challenges of the service industry, I looked forward to going to work each morning.

During the drive to my second job, I would begin to feel down and oppressed. I would arrive at the shadowy warehouse to a crew who acted more like prisoners than the healthy young men they were. The occasional banter they engaged in consisted of criticism of the managers, degrading comments about women, and sarcastic digs at one another. In terms of human relationships, it was a transition from light to dark, from connection to conflict, from peace to wartime.

I had ruined my reputation during my first days at the warehouse by carrying over my state of mind from the deli. I was labeled in a variety of negative ways for my positive mood and became a target for criticism and the scapegoat for random things that went wrong. I was regularly given the most difficult physical assignments and was often ignored when I would try to participate in the conversation. Even though I was an adult, I found myself being bullied.

The most striking thing for me was the change in my own experience and state of mind as I drove to the warehouse each day. I could feel my spirits deflating and my mood darken, and I experienced actual physical pain in my chest and stomach.

The stark contrast between my experience of myself in the mornings and evenings made me confused as to my own identity. Which of these two people was me?

In the midst of my confusion, I discovered how much power the way people treat us has in determining our state of mind and body. It is clear that we are social organisms attuned to the behaviors and emotions of those around us. This means that our identities are, in part, built by relationships. In considering the power of social attunement, we need to consider the many types of relationships that make up a school community.

Just as my coworkers impacted my experiences, teachers and administrators have the power to modulate the brains of students and shape their social instincts in the service of learning. Good educational relationships increase optimism, self-esteem, and well-being while supporting cognitive and emotional development. On the other hand, bad relationships impede social, emotional, and cognitive development, leading to decreased academic success. An intense dedication to attachment-based teaching becomes increasingly important as we focus on students in failing schools within impoverished communities. These students need the extra attention and support of a tribal classroom.

Physical health, mental well-being, and positive social connectedness are highly correlated, strong scientific evidence for the fundamental unity of mind, body, and our social brains. Social support buffers us against stress while reducing blood pressure, stress hormone levels, autonomic and cardiovascular reactivity, and the risk of illness. Social support also facilitates the production of protein-based molecules like T cells and natural killer cells that promote immune functioning. In addition to psychological benefits, a tribal classroom can also improve the physical health of your students. This means more time spent in the classroom.

The Impact of Social Stress

To him who is in fear, everything rustles.

Sophocles

Although many of us are aware of the importance of positive relationships in the classroom, most of us are unaware of the negative relationships that our students may be navigating at home, on the schoolyard, and in the streets. Many children suffer abuse and *bullying* in silence, with only a few dramatic and lethal cases making the news. Bullies and abusers keep silent for fear of reprimand while victims remain silent out of shame and fear of reprisal. I remember the terror of being the target of a bully and the shame of not doing anything to help other victims.

Dominance displays are more frequent during the formation of new groups. This is why bullying is more likely to occur at the beginning of secondary school and in the first week of summer camp. Most incidents of bullying are meant to be witnessed and remembered by group members. On average, four peers witness episodes of adolescent bullying, and they are usually passive or participate in the bullying. Preteen bystanders are almost always present yet seldom intervene. Adolescent bystanders tend to identify with the victims and may even experience vicarious trauma. As we will see, being bullied can cause psychological and physical problems that can last a lifetime.

Bullying is a strategy of establishing social dominance that demonstrates a high degree of similarity among monkeys, chimps, apes, and humans. In other primates, bullying is displayed in behaviors like charging, pounding the chest, and bellowing. Given our more sophisticated brain, bullying in humans has expanded to include teasing, name calling, stealing, taunting, humiliating, spreading rumors, attacks through social media, and social exclusion.

Imagine how a young boy might feel as he prepares to leave home to walk to school, knowing that he won't be safe again until he gets home that afternoon. He looks over his shoulder, jumps at any loud noise, and quickens his pace when the bullies or gang bangers come into view. Although getting to class makes him feel a little safer, he has to be careful not to look like he is smart or cooperating with the teacher lest he attract unwanted attention.

It takes a lot of energy to survive the stress of getting through the day. In a fundamental way, the victims of bullies are living the lives of animals of prey, constantly vigilant for stronger and more aggressive animals capable of doing them harm. Not surprisingly, bullied students have increased anxiety and elevated stress hormone levels right before lunch and at the end of the day as they brace themselves to leave the relative safety of the classroom.

While the bodily changes that occur in victims of bullying have not been studied, we do know what happens in animals when exposed to their natural predators. Rats exposed to the sight, sounds, or smells of cats show all of the signs of fear including startle, freezing, and retreat. The processes of learning and memory are inhibited and exploration comes to a halt. Being in danger disrupts at least a dozen biochemical processes related to learning and memory, creating a significant handicap in the classroom and in life. While we cannot know everything that goes on inside our students, strong tribal bonds make it more likely that they will share their struggles with us.

Bullies and their Victims

*A man can fail many times, but he isn't a failure until he begins to
blame somebody else.*

John Burroughs

Being bullied can have serious emotional and behavioral consequences, especially if it is extreme or chronic. Studies have
shown that victimization results in depression, anxiety, sleep disturbance, and even symptoms of post-traumatic stress disorder.
In fact, 17% of gays, lesbians, and bisexuals who experienced
chronic bullying during adolescence continue to experience
symptoms of post-traumatic stress in adulthood. Any and all of
these symptoms of anxiety will affect children's ability to learn
by undermining their attention, concentration, and memory.

Sadly, the children who most need acceptance, those who
suffer from depression, have low self-esteem, and demonstrate
poor social skills, are most likely to be bullied. Kids who are
overweight, less physically attractive, or suffer with problems at
home are all common targets. Boys tend to suffer physical
attacks while girls experience victimization via gossip, criticism,
attacks on social media, and social exclusion. Being bullied
increases stress hormone levels, impairs memory functioning,
and impedes learning. Bullying also increases the frequency of
illnesses that increase time out of class and social isolation.
Because of its prevalence and impact on the brain and body,
the identification and prevention of bullying has become a
central issue in education.

The Results of Being Bullied

- Anxiety, depression, and suicidal ideation
- Sleep disturbance, loneliness, and helplessness
- Emotional numbing, illness, and absenteeism

While far less research has been done in the area of cyber-bullying, the causes and consequences parallel face-to-face bullying. Up to half of all children surveyed reported at least one incident of being cyberbullied with many victims not knowing the identity of the perpetrator. Absences, suspensions, and carrying a gun to school have been linked to being harassed online.

As you might expect, those children likely to become bullies are also at risk for a variety of psychosocial and academic difficulties. They have a greater likelihood of being victims of abuse, poor attachment relationships, depression, and suicide. Children and adolescents who bully others are likely to have parents who bully them, and they are likely unskilled at emotional communication. Bullies are also at increased risk for future psychological problems, suggesting that bullying is a cry for help.

A warm and supportive family environment helps to buffer victims from the impacts of bullying, and it also reduces the risk that a child will become a bully. This likely holds true for a secure classroom environment, which serves as a safe emotional haven for students. A tribal classroom also allows for the building of alliances for students who may be unable to forge social bonds in the broader school environment. These positive relationships in the classroom may buffer them against the likelihood of being bullied in silence outside of the classroom.

Adults Bullying Adults

We must not allow other people's limited perceptions to define us.
                                                        Virginia Satir

Bullying between adults is surprisingly common. In fact, a quarter of working adults report being bullied at work via social exclusion, criticism, and having their work or reputation sabotaged. Bullied adults often dread going to work in the morning and come to feel physically ill as they approach the job site. It is likely that many develop physical illnesses, take stress leave, or leave the field altogether.

Workplace bullying results in the same demoralization, anxiety, depression, and poor physical health experienced by child and adolescent victims. Some teachers may be easy targets for scapegoating because they stand out in some way, have lower status, or are less able to defend themselves. Young and idealistic teachers are at particular risk for being criticized, and they are more vulnerable to being scapegoated for systemic failures. In a similar dynamic, highly successful teachers report being the targets of anger and jealously from their peers.

It took us years to take student bullying seriously, and we now need to turn our attention to these destructive interactions between adults. Many teachers feel bullied by their principals and coworkers. Administrators and everyone on a faculty should adopt the same zero-tolerance stance toward bullying and shaming interactions among teachers and staff as they have with students. Principals, as tribal chiefs, are responsible for watching over and protecting everyone in the school community if a positive tribal environment is to be created and maintained. Focusing on how the adults in your tribe treat one another sends a strong message of care. This message will go right to the heart of primitive social instincts and support the success of your school.

As you improve your teaching skills and build your tribe, you may notice resistance or even hostility from other teachers or administrators. Do not be discouraged. Your students, especially those without strong family bonds, will forever appreciate the opportunity to create a stable tribe in your classroom. If you are concerned about this type of reaction, be prepared by forming close bonds with like-minded colleagues and develop personal strategies that will help you cope with any negativity you may experience.

Teacher Burnout

Many people die at twenty-five and aren't buried until they are seventy-five.

Benjamin Franklin

When teachers feel powerless and isolated, they often become depressed and demoralized, and give up hope. The more a school resembles a rigid bureaucratic hierarchy with undemocratic policies, the greater the chance of teacher *burnout*. While there may not be a particular bully, a teacher may feel bullied or scapegoated by the system itself. The more a principal can buffer teachers from some of the pressures of the system and establish a sense of tribe among faculty and staff, the more teachers will feel satisfied, thrive, and stay in the profession.

> ***Burnout*** is a condition of physical and emotional exhaustion caused by doing a difficult job for a long period of time.

Teachers report much greater job satisfaction when they feel effective, valued, and able to participate in opportunities to learn. On the other hand, the correlates of burnout read like a perfect storm of assaults on self-esteem and emotional well-being. Chronic stress, insufficient support from administrators, challenging students, and a lack of adequate training all contribute to burnout. Consistently low student achievement, despite sustained teacher effort, is a central cause of demoralization.

Teacher Burnout: Systemic Factors

- Lack of adequate resources and facilities
- High-stakes testing and accountability
- Excessive paperwork and other demands
- Low participation in decision making
- Large classes and schools
- Lack of advancement opportunities
- Low organization efficacy
- High organizational rigidity

Like everyone else, teachers struggle to focus on their work and stay sane in poorly managed organizations. Principals who are good managers and who effectively define and communicate the mission of the school promote job satisfaction and decrease burnout. The chance of burnout increases as teachers are cut out of decision-making processes, lack advancement opportunities, and have little control over what they do.

Dealing with verbal abuse, student disrespect, and concerns for one's physical safety promotes emotional exhaustion. Larger chaotic classrooms, combined with greater student apathy and the stress of high-stakes testing, all correlate with burnout. These factors all become amplified in inner-city, low-income schools, with a greater proportion of minority students. These factors contribute to the disparity between educational needs and available resources. The following list summarizes the psychological and social correlates of burnout.

Teacher Burnout: Psychological & Social Factors

- Lack of collegiality, support, and connection
- Being single or divorced
- Low self-management skills

- Low student achievement
- Low self-concept and self-esteem
- Negative student behavior and fear of violence
- Student apathy, indifference, absences
- Low salary, low status, feeling unappreciated
- Lack of assertiveness
- Low self-awareness and openness to change

Teachers suffering from burnout and unteachable students experience high levels of stress and lack a sense of purpose for being in the classroom. As teachers burn out, their tolerance and concern for their students decline and student achievement falls. As this race to the bottom gains momentum, teachers develop callous, cynical attitudes, and they grow increasingly ineffective. They suffer from increasingly poor physical health as their overall quality of life diminishes. These negative interactions create and maintain chronically failing schools.

As you might expect, a lack of social support is highly predictive of burnout. Teachers who are single or divorced, or lack solid social connections outside of work are most vulnerable. Collegiality, positive collaboration, and a flexible interpersonal context allow teachers to cope with the day-to-day struggles by promoting personal and professional satisfaction. The fact that teachers are adult professionals makes no difference when it comes to our basic social instincts to connect, belong, and feel valued. Teachers need compassionate and caring administrators as much as children need those qualities in their teachers.

It takes considerable strength of character, self-esteem, and determination to be a successful teacher. Teachers who succeed, especially in more difficult schools and classrooms, need to be up to the challenge. Those who succeed adapt to these situations, work hard to change them, and utilize others to cope with stress and take on the problems. Those who succeed have the ability to communicate, maintain good relationships, and impact the culture of the school. These teachers are able to summon the energy from within and gain the support from others that creates a sustaining tribal work-around.

Teachers with inadequate social support in their private lives are more vulnerable to burnout. This can be compounded by the presence of fragile defenses that lead them to avoid facing difficulties. Those who end up leaving the profession are characterized by an inactive and passive coping style, unrealistic expectations of others, and a tendency to blame external factors for their difficulties. Teachers who persevere are more confident, possess more direct styles of coping, and actively seek out help and additional training.

The more time teachers devote to proactive classroom management and teaching strategies, the less stress they experience from discipline problems and work overload. Having a conceptual framework for dealing with challenging classrooms and topics provides more practical tools while decreasing the anxiety and other negative emotions involved in dealing with challenging situations. Successful teachers feel competent, satisfied with their work, less stressed, and are ultimately less prone to burnout. Teachers feel most committed to their schools when they see their work as meaningful and are able to achieve positive and meaningful results. The more positive emotions we experience at work, the more resilient and motivated we will be in facing the complex demands of teaching.

The Need for Broader Training

What the teacher is, is more important what he teaches.

Karl A. Menninger

From the start, it is clear that much more is required of teachers than they were expecting or prepared for. Despite the fact that we are called upon to be counselors, social workers, and parents, training programs prepare aspiring teachers only to be instructors. Once on the job, administrators treat teachers as instructors or policemen, emphasizing test scores, grades, attendance, and obedience. The majority of special education teachers report that they left college unprepared to meet the learning needs of diverse students, to balance the demands they had to face, and to cope with the poor working conditions they discovered in the field.

Teachers need to be better prepared by their training programs to understand and deal with the social, emotional, and practical issues they will encounter. The teacher's perceived ability to respond to students' human needs has been shown to have a high correlation with perceived effectiveness as an instructor. How our students respond to us frames our experience of the classroom. After all, our students are our primary social connections at work. When we feel ineffective in reaching our students on a personal level, we often feel helpless, incompetent, and unfulfilled. Therefore, initial teacher training and continuing education should include a strong emphasis on building secure attachments and healthy tribes.

Application Box: Self-Care Take-Home Messages

- Spend time with friends and family who are positive, comforting, and supportive.
- Invest time in establishing professional support groups and connecting with a trusted mentor.
- Actively seek out ongoing training and self-growth opportunities; make them a priority.
- Take time for yourself and remember to do the things that sustain you body, mind, and soul.

Because teachers strive to behave in a professional manner, it is difficult to know how to deal with negative feelings. It is essential, however, for teachers to develop close relationships both in and out of the profession that provide an outlet for all of their emotions. As we saw earlier, avoiding negative emotions increases both stress and burnout. Principals can help by exploring ways to express negative emotions in safe and constructive ways. Teachers can even suggest group activities to relieve stress and to open a dialogue.

Teachers Need a Supportive Tribe and a Wise Chief

It is difficult to give children a sense of security unless you have it yourself. If you have it, they catch it from you.

William Menninger

While successful teaching requires creating a tribal classroom, being a successful principal requires building a tribal school. School cultures that parallel tribal life—those with collegiality, collaboration, and wise leadership—reduce burnout and increase teacher satisfaction. Just as teachers can create environments where students' social instincts are harnessed in the service of learning, principals can shape the culture of the school so that it raises teacher morale and increases efficacy.

Unfortunately, most principals do not focus on how to create and maintain positive school culture. Many fail to create a sense of fairness, provide adequate feedback, or create flexible and successful administrative processes. This is probably why most teachers feel that administrative meetings are unhelpful in solving the problems that they face. Does this sound familiar? Stress and burnout increase when teachers feel that demands are high yet their ability to make changes to enhance success is low. Students will fail as long as we continue to fail our teachers.

Despite enjoying rewarding contact with colleagues, a majority of teachers report that they rarely or never feel a psychological sense of community at their schools. Keep in mind that the correlates of teacher burnout include isolation, feeling incapable of eliciting support from others, and failing to master the social environment. The activation and utilization of primitive social instincts are a big part of the success of smaller schools. They allow for greater intimacy, familiarity, and personal interactions that support academic performance and encourage greater participation in extracurricular activities.

Administrators can strive to create flexible, collaborative, and inclusive school cultures that harness primitive social instincts, dramatically improving teacher morale and performance. Principals promote teacher morale by being good managers and encouraging teachers to collaborate in decision making, which reduces stress, increases job satisfaction, and reduces role ambiguity. Teachers can do their part by participating in staff meetings, contributing ideas, and being more involved. They then have to be met by administrators who know how to listen, be supportive, and share control.

When teachers are in the role of chief in the classroom, giving is expected. Yet when they take on the role of tribal member, the expectation is to be provided for. Studies indicate most teachers passively await the support they long for from principals. A great deal of burnout is due to the perceived disparity between the energy and effort teachers put into schools and what they get back. Consider your own administration and your interactions with the principal, other teachers, or staff members. Do you actively participate in and encourage change? If not, this is an excellent opportunity to become a champion. Pick a project that you feel will improve your school and do everything you can to make it happen.

Whether or not we are successful in adding social and emotional development to the teacher-training curriculum, the need for continuing education, support, and mentorship while in the classroom continue throughout our careers. It is obvious that teachers need a variety of skills that usually fall under the headings of counseling and psychotherapy. And while it may be unrealistic to expect much of this training to occur when they are students, there is no doubt that they and their students could benefit from ongoing exposure to information and the opportunity to practice social and emotional skills into the classroom.

A creative and promising way of accomplishing this goal is through non-profit organizations that can satisfy these needs in ways that the educational system is still unprepared. One such example is FuelEd Schools (also known as FuelEd), that brings together educators and therapists for education, problem-solving sessions, and personal exploration.

FuelEd

Where there is charity and wisdom, there is neither fear nor ignorance.
St. Francis of Assisi

A promising way of building positive learning environments is through the use of external consultants. One such organization, FuelEd, is the brainchild of Megan Marcus. While a graduate student at the Harvard School of Education, she envisioned and began developing a training program that addresses the social and emotional challenges encountered by classroom teachers. Her program is a direct attempt to fill the gap between teacher preparation and the actual job. Here is how Megan describes the mission of FuelEd:

A relationship with a consistent and caring adult provides the conditions for optimal learning and development. Proven outcomes of such relationships include physical regulation, communication skills, emotional balance, flexibility, the ability to self-soothe fear, and the development of insight, empathy, and morality—basically, all qualities we would hope for in our children, our neighbors, ourselves. Unfortunately, half of all children lack these foundational relationship experiences and are therefore at a significant disadvantage in the classroom and in life.

Worse yet, while research has shown that teacher-student relationships can compensate for this, promoting higher academic achievement, greater social competence, and less behavioral problems in students, current educator training focuses narrowly technical teaching skills, excluding a critical dimension of teacher effectiveness: the ability to build and maintain positive relationships.

FuelEd was founded to solve this problem. Our mission is to strengthen educator preparation, quality, and retention by equipping educators with the social and emotional competencies essential for building relationships in schools. We believe that if educators are socially and emotionally equipped, they will remain in their professions longer and develop stronger relationships with all school stakeholders. In turn, these relationships will drive students' academic, social, and emotional learning.

FuelEd builds the foundation for attachment-based learning environments by developing educators' knowledge of the science of relationships, their relationship skills, and the self-awareness necessary to building relationships:

Science of Relationships. FuelEd's interdisciplinary curriculum weaves developmental and counseling psychology together with social neuroscience, exploring questions such as how the brain develops in the context of early relationships, how student behavior is influenced by their relationship history, and most importantly, how the brain continues to develop through relationships—which is where the power of educators lies. Through psychoeducation, activities, and discussion, educators begin to understand that oftentimes students' "misbehavior" is actually attributed to their early relationship history.

This new understanding empowers educators to avoid the trap of personalizing a students' misbehavior ("What's wrong with me?") or blaming a student ("What's wrong with you?"). Instead, educators can conceptualize students in the context of their broader lives and relationship needs—thereby improving their ability to tend to those needs. Providing a new way to think about relationships is one of the intended outcomes of FuelEd's program, as research has indicated that teachers' mental representations of student relationships predicts academic performance and adjustment in school.

Skills of Relationships. There are a variety of relationship skills that contribute to our ability to be secure attachment figures. As such, skill building is a large component of FuelEd's program. FuelEd aims to help educators move away from relationship behaviors that promote insecure attachment (i.e. shaming, modeling unhealthy ways of dealing with emotions, or being unresponsive to other's needs or emotions) and towards relationship behaviors that promote secure attachment (i.e. being aware of and responsive to others feelings, expressing feelings in healthy and appropriate way, and showing unconditional acceptance). After all, it is those moments when a teacher stops and provides empathy and understanding, refraining from problem solving or reassuring, that ultimately builds a students' brain in addition to their self-regulation, self-awareness, self-reliance, and self esteem.

Self-Awareness of Relationships. Teachers, like students, are not blank slates. Educators have a history of relationships, which shape their thoughts, feelings, and behavior in relationships with others. In fact, studies have shown that adults differ in their ability to develop consisting, caring relationships with children according to their own relationship history. Those who experienced secure attachments are more able to respond sensitively and appropriately to a child's needs than adults with insecure attachments in their past. But research has also shown there is an exciting exception to this rule: when adults develop an awareness of their personal stories and experience subsequent secure relationships, they are able to successfully build secure attachments with others—regardless of their relationship histories.

If educators are to promote secure attachment in others, they must be securely attached which means their training must include, not only the science or the skills of relationships, but an exploration of the self. FuelEd's One-on-Ones provide educators with the opportunity to engage in safe, supportive, and secure relationships with FuelEd Counselors that foster personal and professional growth. Other benefits of One-on-Ones include stress and emotion reduction, increased awareness of personal triggers, and improvement of general satisfaction and interpersonal skills.

In short, we see that if we want our education system to develop whole students, teachers need so much more than content knowledge and instructional skills. The key to students' learning and development rests in the educators' emotional intelligence, emotional availability, emotional health, and way of being in a relationship. All educators should be equipped to provide a model for what a secure relationship can be. Many do this naturally, but for those who don't, the best news of all is that the same way that students grow, learn, develop and change in the face of new, secure relationship, so can adults.

(Used with permission of Megan Marcus)

For more information on FuelEd, visit: www.fueledschools.com.

Exercise 6: Teacher Self-Assessment—Am I Being Bullied?

Programs to raise awareness and prevent bullying in children and adolescents are everywhere, and I suspect that you have already been exposed to at least one. Even if there are school-wide antibullying programs, I strongly suggest that you spend some time in the classroom updating and reinforcing the principles and practices that have been instituted by your school. Within the classroom tribe, you have the opportunity to make these insights more immediate and personal.

Although antibullying programs for students are everywhere, I have yet to see any programs designed to raise awareness and improve the behaviors of teachers. We spend almost no formal time examining how teachers are bullied by coworkers, administrators, and aspects of the system.

This is a *self-assessment,* using the principles of this chapter, that goes beyond bullying to an assessment of the quality of your life.

After reading this chapter, you now know that bullying impacts thoughts, feelings, and behaviors—usually for the worse. Sometimes it is really obvious that you are being bullied while at other times, it is a subtle process that may creep up on you. It may be beneficial to take a personal inventory about how you feel about the quality of your work experiences, relationships, and health. It is important to take this inventory a few times a year.

Let's start with what happens when we are bullied.

- Am I experiencing feelings of anxiety, depression, loneliness, numbing, or helplessness?
- How is my sleep? Appetite? Energy level?
- Do I get sick more often, withdraw socially, or not enjoy things that were once pleasurable?

Next, think about the quality of your daily experiences in your school.

- **My classroom:** Do I have adequate resources, a reasonable number of students, and a positive and safe classroom environment? Does it feel like my students care and are motivated to learn?
- **My career:** Do the expectations placed on me match the challenges and resources I am provided; do I participate in decision making, and do I have opportunities for career advancement? Do I make enough money? Do I feel appreciated?
- **My colleagues:** Do I have the respect of my colleagues? Am I connected to and supported by my colleagues? Does my principal have a clear mission and run my school in a well-organized, flexible, and efficient manner?
- **My personal life:** Do I have good relationships with family, friends, colleagues, and significant others? Do I feel good about myself and my life? Do I feel that I know and like myself?

There is no score to determine whether you are enjoying your life and your work. The answer about whether you are swimming or drowning in your life is highly personal. The central issue is to assess the quality of your work and life experience. Either way, you are bringing your emotional reality into the classroom every day—for better and worse. If you do feel bullied, it is important to take immediate action. You can consult a therapist to assist you with these problems.

PART III

Turning Brains On to Learning

CHAPTER 7

Being Seen and Feeling Felt

Courage starts with showing up and letting ourselves be seen.
                                        Brené Brown

*T*he central elements of emotional intelligence are awareness *of our inner worlds and a curiosity about what is going on in the hearts and minds of others. Humans have evolved to be highly sensitive to others and there is no doubt that we have the ability to influence the inner states of those around us. As authority figures and surrogate parents, teachers have a direct line to the brains of our students. Because of this responsibility, we have to learn about our conscious and unconscious feelings because of their influence on our students and the culture of the classroom.*

Our brains have been shaped to watch, listen, and attune to those around us. We imitate the behaviors and resonate with the emotions of others in ways that weave us together into couples, families, and tribes. Much of this occurs through reflexive, fast, and largely unconscious processes.

The mechanisms of imitation and emotional attunement remained a mystery until a clue was accidentally discovered in a research lab in Milan. Neurons in the cortex of primates were discovered to fire both when a primate observed a researcher engaging in a specific behavior and when the primate engaged in the identical behavior. These neurons were so finely tuned that they fired only when a specific object was grasped by particular fingers in a certain way. Actions such as picking up a banana with the right hand at a specific angle, peeling it with the thumb and forefinger, or bringing it to the mouth were found to activate specific neurons.

It became obvious that these neurons were involved in the action because they didn't fire in response to the hand, the banana, or the two presented together. They fired only when the hand was acting on the banana in a particular way to attain a certain goal. These cells came to be called *mirror neurons,* and their existence reflects the fact that we evolved to learn from important others through observation and imitation.

Mirror neurons connect sensory, motor, and emotional brain circuits, which allows for learning through observation, better group coordination, and predicting the behaviors of others. Connections with emotional circuitry allow us to get a sense of what is in the heart of another person by simulating in our bodies through what we see, hear, and feel them communicating to us across the social synapse.

Mirror neurons evolved as a way for behaviors to automatically transfer from one animal to another across the social synapse. When one primate watches another performing an action, such as breaking the hard shell of a nut between two rocks, the motor circuits in the observer's brain needed to perform the same action become activated. It then connects these behaviors with the attainment of a goal (in this case eating), serving to motivate and reinforce the behavioral sequence leading to it. In this way, our brains actually practice doing what we are watching in order to imitate these behaviors to attain the same reward. This is why imitation is such a powerful learning tool in the classroom.

Physical Imitation and Bodily Activation

From caring comes courage.

Lao Tzu

Newborns begin to imitate the facial expressions of adults just hours after birth. When adults open their mouths, stick out their tongues, or make happy or sad faces, babies reflexively imitate their actions. Looking up when we see others doing it and yawning in response to the yawns of others are examples of reflexive imitation that continue throughout life. Why has evolution selected the automatic imitation of facial expressions, gestures, and actions? The most likely explanation is that imitation is central to interpersonal attunement and group coordination.

Many think that mirror neurons were vital to the evolution of language by connecting individuals through grasping, sharing, and using objects together. This evolved into hand gestures representing certain words, behaviors, and states of mind, and eventually into the symbolic code of spoken language. You can see the continued interconnection between spoken language and gestures by observing the number of hand and body gestures that accompany speech. Watching someone give directions over the phone while using hand gestures demonstrates that these actions are more for the sender than the receiver.

A gesture can be more than just a single word; it can also represent a set of movements, intentions, and requests. For example, imagine a teenager who spots a friend on a passing escalator going the other way. She can hold her hand to her head, extending fingers to her mouth and ear to let him know that she wants him to call her. If she shakes her hand rapidly with emphasis and widens her eyes, she also lets him know that she wants this to happen: "Oh my God! Really, really soon!" Thus, the gesture of an action (talking on the phone) becomes a prefix for a set of actions and a desired outcome.

It seems clear that our problem-solving abilities are derived not from abstract logic but from interactions with the physical environment. This helps us to understand why active teachers who use movement with their lessons are often so successful. Because we imitate those we like more than those we don't, establishing positive relationships makes it more likely our lessons will be imitated and remembered by our students. In a tribal classroom, secure attachment is a direct line to your students' hearts, minds, and brains via mirror neurons.

Although the implications of mirror neurons for classroom teaching are many, there are a few key points to keep in mind: (1) our students learn as much from watching the example we set as from the materials we teach; (2) students attune to our inner emotional states and are often aware of our feelings before we are; and (3) a positive emotional environment in the classroom will change their brains, minds, and biochemistries.

We ask students to treat each other with respect, but if we are disrespectful to them or if they see us disrespecting others, they learn both lessons. Experience shows that, especially under stress, they will do as we do, not as we say.

There are three clear take-home messages here: (1) pay attention to your facial expressions, postures, and tone of voice because they have a powerful influence on the emotional climate of the class; (2) make sure to take care of yourself and enjoy life because your students will feel your exhaustion, sadness, or despair even if they are your secrets; and (3) practice what you preach.

Emotional Attunement and Congruent Communication

You must be the change you wish to see in the world.

Unknown

As we evolved, the functions of mirror neurons expanded to connect neural networks dedicated to imitation with those responsible for social and emotional processing. This advancement paved the way for emotional attunement, compassion, and empathy. Linkage of mirror systems to those dedicated to emotion now allows us to map what we see others experience onto our own nervous systems. When we look at another's face, muscles in our own face become activated in imitation of the perceived expressions.

Seeing a child cry makes us reflexively frown, tilt our heads, say "aawww," and feel sad. Watching a defeated athlete walk slowly off the field leads us to feel deflated and may even trigger personal memories of disappointment and loss. In these and countless other ways, mirror neurons, and the neural systems they connect, bridge the gap between sender and receiver, enhancing emotional attunement and understanding.

Mothers rely on mirror systems to stay emotionally attuned to their children. The quality of mother-child emotional resonance will correlate with the child's later functioning, including time spent in social engagement, emotional regulation, symbolic play, verbal IQ, and overall emotional intelligence. Emotional attunement also has a downside; it makes us susceptible to being infected by the negative feelings of others. This is why both joy and depression feel contagious and why fears, anxieties, and phobias can be passed from one person to another. Emotions spread via facial expressions, bodily postures, words, deeds, and beliefs. A teacher's stress, fatigue, and anger will also resonate within students via the same mirror systems.

Listening With Your Third Ear

We have two ears and one tongue so that we would listen more and talk less.

Diogenes

Everyone should be listened to on a regular basis. However, when I ask students if they have someone who really knows how to listen, a little less than half are able to think of one person. When I ask the same students how many people they know, they'll say "hundreds." The fact is that while many people are good at talking, very few are good at listening. Teachers who can learn to listen gain a powerful relationship tool and the opportunity to connect with many students who are desperately in need of a good ear.

Students who know how to listen are more likely to learn, develop deeper relationships, and come to better know themselves. I believe that we can learn how to teach by first finding out what makes our students feel listened to, heard, and understood. If you can give this gift to your students, they will mirror it and pay it forward. Just counting slowly to five in your head before responding gives the other person time to say more while having the experience that what he or she said is more important to you than your response.

When you are listening to others, imagine your heart as a third ear. Use it to pay attention to the emotions behind the words being said. Think of your body as a satellite dish picking up faint vibrations from within your students and see if you can translate them into words that can be shared with them. Try to avoid becoming a detective in getting to the source of your students' feelings. Simply attune to what is being experienced and let them know that you get their feelings. This usually allows them to talk less and say more. In other words, students become less concerned with the flood of details that usually surround, obscure, and justify feelings; instead they get to the heart of the matter.

For most of us, learning to listen and engaging in congruent communication does not come naturally. It is an achievement that takes time and a great deal of practice (Ginott, 1972). While teachers are given almost no training in basic communication and empathy skills, it is this ability that will gain the most leverage with students struggling to learn in the midst of the struggles of growing up. The truth is we are only able to deal with the emotions of others to the degree that we are open to our own emotions. If we are trying to keep our own emotions at bay, we may miss the most important aspects of our students' experiences. Here is a teacher who learned how to make her students' emotions part of the learning experience.

Tears for Freshman Comp

By Lisa Shapiro

I always shed tears at funerals, weddings, or a dedication ceremony to name a baby. One other place I'm almost certain to cry is in my freshman composition class. When I first started teaching college English, I was stunned to discover how many students hated it, and their loathing of the subject seemed directly connected to past experience with the five-paragraph essay. This simple structure—an introductory paragraph followed by three body paragraphs with a topic sentence and supporting examples, and then a paragraph of conclusion—helps students organize information. As a creative process, however, it's like spending a few hours naked in a walk-in freezer—mind-numbing to the point of imaginative hypothermia.

To rekindle the fire of inspiration, I asked my students to write narrative essays. My goal was to get them to hear their own voice—the "I" voice—which many of them had been cautioned never to use in writing. What ensued was like a reality TV show for freshman comp, with everyone spilling all kinds of emotional stuff; to hell with the punctuation. Then, to help students really hear their writing voice, I asked them to read their essays out loud.

This process of writing and reading seemed to draw them out, to help them connect to the class and to one another. The students also became more engaged with the content of their essays, and they seemed willing to pay a little more attention to details like sentence structure. Initially, I thought this was just a backdoor approach to essay writing, a way to get them to buy into the assignment by making it more relevant to their own experience. Gradually, however, I began to see that in addition to being more interested intellectually, the students were also more engaged emotionally, which led them to take more control of the assignment. Rather than waiting for instructions, they would often approach to ask if they could tackle a certain topic.

Could they write about getting drunk, stealing, using drugs, being involved in a gang? The answer was yes—always yes. Could they use swear words? Of course. Not all of my students were rascals; some wrote about sitting in a hospital room with a parent who had cancer, and then becoming like a parent to a younger sibling. They wrote about loss and love and life, and about all the lessons they learned. At some point, the essay itself took a back seat to the topic, and it seemed to me that that was how it should be—content should dictate structure.

Something else was happening in the classroom, too, and after a while I couldn't ignore it any longer. The essays that my students were writing were important to them, and they were important to me, and not just as a teaching tool. Their words got under my skin, wormed their way into my consciousness and into my heart. Their lessons left a mark on me, and I was learning from their experiences. I wasn't immune to the emotional vulnerability they shared, and so the classroom was suddenly a riskier place for me to be. It caused me pain, and it made me cry.

These moments that I share with my students are as beautiful as they are painful; they impact me as much as any wedding or funeral, and they happen every semester. I know that when I walk into a classroom and students start writing and reading their stories, their lessons will open me, fracture and enlighten me. Freshman comp is one of those classes that students dread, but it's the class where I learn the most, and I've come to love it, even though it makes me cry.

(Used with permission of Lisa Shapiro)

Emotional Contagion

When a hundred men stand together, each of them loses his mind and gets another one.

Nietzsche

The fact that human brains are social organs is apparent every time we witness an emotion spread through a classroom. Many students are tuned into subtle, unconscious social signals, and they are especially sensitive to the emotions of others. This is often true for people who grow up having to contend with unpredictable or dangerous parents or communities. Some people develop such extreme sensitivity to others that they come to believe that they have clairvoyant abilities. The importance of emotional contagion to survival is likely related to the coordination of social behavior and the benefits of shared emotions to establish loyalty to the group.

Imitative behaviors, like yawning or looking up when you see others doing it, help to coordinate group behavior, but they also make us more susceptible to the influences of the group mind and mob behavior. The emotional expressions of those with whom we interact also impact our social judgment.

For example, people are more likely to vote for a candidate if a newscaster describes the candidate with a smile. Positive and negative emotions ripple through groups; fearful facial expressions will make others orient in the direction of the gaze, providing rapid communication about a potential danger. All of these instincts and reflexes are at work in the classroom.

Other, less benign forms of emotional contagion include trauma and suicide. Suicides of celebrities often trigger copycats, especially in adolescents who have overidentified with them. Like sadness and suicide, laughter is also contagious, which makes us laugh more when watching a funny movie with a group or when a laugh track is added to a soundtrack. Positive emotional contagion within a group enhances cooperation and task performance while decreasing conflict. This is why the use of humor can be so helpful in the classroom.

Application Box

It may be helpful to start the day with positive affirmations. This will focus your students, create a positive attitude, and acknowledge your expectations for the classroom. Take a few minutes in the morning for your students to recite an affirmation as a group. Here is an example, but you can adjust affirmations for your purposes, goals, and the age of your students: "We are a tribe. We will all work together to achieve our goals. We will protect and support each other. We affirm that we are all equal and capable. We will work to create the best classroom so that we will all succeed."

There are also aspects of emotional contagion that are best described as inspiration—the kind we hope to foster in our classrooms. There are people capable of inspiring us to change our thinking, have courage in the face of danger, and behave in new and more life-affirming ways. Think of the young man in Tiananmen Square standing in front of the advancing tanks, Rosa Parks refusing to surrender her seat on a bus, or Winston Churchill's radio addresses during the bombing of London. These words and deeds warm our hearts and make us reconsider our acceptance of the status quo. This visceral reaction to the inspirational behavior of others is another aspect of emotional contagion that serves group coherence and positive change.

Application Box

Share stories of your heroes with your students and describe why you think they were so courageous. Then have your students list their own heroes. Ask your students what makes these people heroes. As a class, discuss how you can all inspire each other. What acts of courage can you engage in every day?

The Power of Attitude

The way is in the heart.

The Buddha

One of the many ways we impact the brains and minds of others is by our expectations of them. Optimism, encouragement, or giving someone the benefit of the doubt have been shown to positively impact performance. Just as significantly, negative biases, prejudices, and disapproval impede learning and performance. Teachers can positively influence the learning, health, and well-being of their students by having positive attitudes about them as people as well as their ability to learn. We can harness the power of emotional attunement in the service of our students through compassionate actions, optimistic attitudes, and kind words. Successful teachers repeatedly demonstrate that positive expectancies beget effort, optimism, and success.

Despite years of training, teachers are humans first and professionals second. This means that our prejudices, moods, and changing states of mind all influence how we relate to others. Our conscious desire to be free of bias doesn't prevent our brains from distorting information in countless ways. The unfortunate fact is that we react differently to students if they are attractive or unattractive, male or female, tall or short, black or white, thin or fat. Although we may think of them as character flaws, these reactive biases are built into the way our brains operate. Character comes into play in recognizing and becoming actively committed to decreasing our prejudices.

For example, middle-class teachers have lower academic expectations for children from lower-income families, and students with lighter skin are seen as higher achievers than those with darker skin. When teachers score exams of allegedly brighter children, their answers are evaluated as having a higher intellectual quality than the exact same work thought to have been done by a "dull" child. Although many biases are mediated by culture, the fact that biases exist is a consequence of having a brain that has evolved to react in a stereotyped manner in order to make quick decisions based on less information. No matter how bright we are, our brains are masters at generating misinformation.

Teacher expectation is an extremely active agent in student achievement. In addition to emotional resonance, expectations are transmitted via social comparison and students' perceptions of a teacher's behaviors toward achievers. Students perceive teachers as giving low achievers more direction, rules, and negative feedback while high achievers receive more opportunities and choice of tasks. These behaviors appear to communicate their implicit expectations of student abilities, thereby influencing student motivation and self-image.

The roots of bias lie in everything from our genetic histories to our cultural context and our personal experiences. And despite the fact that most of us would like to think that we are without prejudice, just the opposite is true. All of us are biased in favor of better-looking, smarter, and wealthier others—our students included. These biases exist despite our conscious beliefs to the contrary. This is both humbling and unsettling news. The first step in decreasing bias is to take its existence for granted and then work on internal and external ways to minimize and eliminate whatever you find.

Reflection Box

Take a moment to think back to a time when you have felt judged based on your race, nationality, the color of your hair, the way you speak, and so on. It doesn't have to be a memory of something obvious. It could also be a sense you had of being viewed in an unfair or biased manner. Once you find an experience, reflect on how it made you feel—angry, ashamed, hopeless, sad, and anxious are all possibilities. Next, consider the impact that these feelings would have on your ability to feel calm and safe as a student sitting in class.

In his research on the power of teacher expectancy, Robert Rosenthal and his colleagues administered traditional IQ tests to students under the guise of the Harvard Test of Inflected Acquisition. The experimenters suggested to the teachers that this test would indicate which students would blossom in the upcoming year and which would fall behind. Twenty percent of the students were randomly selected as the "bloomers," and this was shared with their teachers. After eight months, the randomly chosen bloomers showed greater gains in IQ and reasoning, and were rated as more intellectually curious, better adjusted, happier, and less needy for approval than the students in the control group. The teachers' expectancies turned into self-fulfilling prophecies. This study and others replicating its basic results are powerful evidence for the fact that how we view our students directly impacts their performance.

Am I a Learner or a Loser?

Excellence is not an act, but a habit.

Will Durant

Students construct their academic self-concept based on how they believe their parents, teachers, and peers appraise their academic ability. Someone with a history of academic success may see a failing grade or teacher negativity as an aberration and shrug it off while someone with a history of failure may experience the same messages as an affirmation of his or her inadequacy. It has been shown that low marks or reading grade placement have less of an effect on children's academic expectations and self-concept than socially transmitted expectations. Students appear to see their academic abilities through their teachers' eyes, working up or down to the level of their teachers' expectation of them.

Mirror neurons that allow for emotional attunement and learning through social imitation have at least as much power for good as for harm. Teachers' unspoken beliefs about students, a class, and their own career get communicated and influence learning outcomes. In the process, teacher expectations and emotions become woven into the fabric of students' academic self-concept and their broader sense of self. A negative academic self-concept has been correlated with a variety of factors including self-defeating attitude, anxiety, and a lack of self-esteem.

Positive academic self-concept is associated with:

- Higher academic achievement
- Greater engagement
- Mastery goal orientation
- Intrinsic motivation
- Persistence
- Goal setting
- Greater effort
- More help-seeking
- Persistence after failure

Unfortunately, the students most likely to receive these negative messages from teachers are those at greatest risk for academic failure. Students with previously poor academic achievement, low self-concept, and those from disadvantaged socioeconomic backgrounds have all been shown to be more vulnerable to the effects of teacher expectations. To make matters worse, the same students are more likely to be in classrooms that test the teacher's competence, morale, and emotional well-being (due to large numbers of students and inadequate teaching resources). On the other hand, these are also the students who most need and benefit from positive emotions and expectations from their teachers. Think back to Marva Collins, who told her students they were brilliant and refused to let them fail.

Protecting Students From Our Conscious and Unconscious Biases

When truth is replaced by silence, the silence is a lie.

Yevgeny Yevtushenko

So what can we do to minimize our natural human biases? Studies have shown that creating more learning independence is a way to help buffer students against teacher expectancy. Variations in teacher expectations appear to be less visible in open classrooms that facilitate student choice of activity, curriculum, and physical space. Offering choices of learning activities, encouraging independent problem solving, or involving students in decision making can increase student independence. These and other learning strategies promote the intrinsic motivation, self-determination, and self-evaluation related to success and failure.

Opportunities for progress, feedback, peer-to-peer teaching, and self-evaluation have also been shown to lessen the effects of teacher attitudes. Students in these open classrooms are more likely to interpret a teacher's negative expectations as feedback and respond with increased effort. Those of us who are more controlling in our teaching styles may find it difficult to establish an autonomous classroom. Not surprisingly, those of us who are least comfortable with student independence may be precisely those who should make the effort.

We all differ in our need to be in control, and I'm sure you've noticed family, friends, and colleagues ranging from laid back to control freak. Where we fall on this control spectrum is a mixture of innate disposition and past experiences, which is heavily influenced by uncertainty, anxiety, and fear. In fact, control is a need to feel safe, secure, and accepted. I certainly know that when I'm anxious about teaching a class or giving a lecture, my first instinct is to overprepare. In contrast,

I've found that the more I relax and share control with students, the better we all feel. Because we often fool ourselves
into believing all kinds of things about ourselves, it might be
good to ask a trusted friend where you fit on the control spectrum—you may be surprised.

Finally, we have to accept that our brains are imperfect.
Accepting this reality instead of denying our limitations allows
us to be open to new learning and provides our students with a
model of openness, humility, and tolerance.

Exercise 7:
Exercising Empathy

The focus of this exercise is to practice empathy—what it means and how to deepen our empathic abilities. The theme of this exercise is being heard and feeling felt. I'll leave it up to you to decide if you feel your students are old enough to engage in this exercise.

The first step is to discuss the definition of empathy and distinguish it from other ways of connecting. Here is my definition: Empathy is a hypothesis (idea or guess) about what others experience. Our hypothesis is based on a combination of what we know about them, the situation they are in, and how we might feel if we were in their place.

It is important to distinguish empathy from the sympathy or compassion that we may feel for them. While important information, sympathy and compassion are our own feelings, and we should not assume they are shared in total or even in part.

Empathy requires humility for at least two reasons. The first is that in order to better understand what someone is experiencing, we have to be quiet and listen. We have to have the ability to enter a state of mind where what is happening is not about us. For some, this is not as easy as it sounds. Second, because empathy is a hypothesis, it is always a guess and should not be presented from the presumptuous position: "I know exactly how you feel!" In this exercise, students will practice these two skills—listening and making empathic statements.

The best way to begin is with a demonstration. Have two volunteers come to the front of the room and sit across from one another. The first step is to have one student (teller) describe a difficult or challenging situation to the other for a couple of minutes. Step two is to have the listener describe the story back to the teller without distortions, additions, or subtractions. The goal of the assignment is met when the teller feels that he or she has been heard and understood by the listener.

The next step is to have the listener make an empathic statement about the internal emotional experience of the teller. The teller can then give feedback about how well the empathic hypothesis matched his or her inner experience. If it is right on, wonderful. If it needs adjustment, encourage the teller to make some suggestions and have the listener take another crack at it. The goal is for the teller to feel felt.

Once this is accomplished, have the teller and listener change roles and repeat the exercise in front of the class. Once this has been accomplished, divide the class up into pairs and have them practice with each other. Float through the room and eavesdrop on interactions to offer guidance and support.

After each pair has had time to repeat the exercise they have just witnessed, come back into the large group and share experiences. At some point in the discussion, identify difficulties experienced by the pairs to see if there are common problems and list them on the board for further discussion.

This exercise can lead in to a more general discussion triggered by the following questions:

- What important person in your life really listens to you? How does that feel?
- What important person in your life doesn't listen to you? How does that feel?
- Who really gets you and how does it feel?

CHAPTER 8

Play, Explore, and Learn

Imagination is more important than knowledge.

Albert Einstein

Exploration and play are reflexive human drives embedded deep in our genes. They are nature's strategies to stimulate the brain to adapt to the ongoing changes in our social and physical worlds. The term "neural plasticity" refers to the ability of neurons and neural networks to be born, grow, and change the way they relate to one another in response to experience. Teachers are in the business of changing the brain—we are the merchants of neuroplasticity. The more we encourage exploration and build play into our teaching, the more easily our students' brains will be turned on to learning.

The classroom is a relatively new phenomenon. For all of prehistory, education was a natural by-product of living. Our compulsion to explore and play is an innate mechanism designed to stimulate our brains to learn adaptive behaviors. This is why we don't need to be rewarded to play—our neurobiology makes sure that it is self-reinforcing. Have you tried to get a seven-year-old out of the pool or to give up the iPad? In many ways, the structure of contemporary education is contrary to these natural learning impulses. Sitting still, paying silent attention to a teacher, and focusing on abstract concepts are unnatural acts.

Learning through play is well accepted in kindergarten. There is also great respect for differences in interests, levels of development, and personal expression. Students roll around on the floor, play games, and are guided to cooperate with each other. Most of all, they are encouraged to use their imaginations, and they are reinforced for coming up with alternative solutions. Drawing ears disconnected from the body is likened to Picasso's later works instead of being a sign of laziness or intellectual problems. Classrooms are designed to stimulate students and draw them into engagement.

These basic human realities and ways of learning are soon forgotten as focus shifts to more passive forms of learning, conformity, and competition. This loss of the spirit of kindergarten is unfortunate (Meier, 2002). In fact, many modern corporations are attempting to change the working environment in line with this spirit in order to encourage creativity, reduce work stress, and improve morale. This attitude began in high-tech companies and slowly spread to other industries. Perhaps every school should be like a start-up business, where those in control are not tied to rigid ideas and rules but, like a tribe, re-create the learning environment in reaction to the day-to-day realities of life.

Enriched, challenging environments result in more resilient brains, which contain more neurons, more complex connections, and greater resilience to stress. In addition, stimulating environments turbocharge the metabolic support systems that nurture and protect the brain. The effects of environmental stimulation on brain growth are robust. One study of Korean children adopted by families in the United States found that environmental enrichment counteracted the effects of early malnutrition and deprivation. These children eventually surpassed Korean averages for height and weight while their IQ scores reached or exceeded averages for American children (Winick, Katchadurian, & Harris, 1975).

Older adults with higher-quality educations and more stimulating occupations have been shown to be better able to cope with the effects of age and brain disease. One explanation, the cognitive reserve hypothesis, asserts that the more brain you build throughout life, the more you can afford to lose as you age while still being able to process information in a competent manner. Executive functions, such as the verbal fluency, controlled processing, and abstract thinking demanded by high-complexity occupations, appear to contribute most to cognitive reserve. These are precisely the challenges we work so hard to present to students in the classroom.

Studies have also found that intellectual decline can be halted or reversed in many older adults by increasing environmental and social stimulation. When faced with a challenging environment, brains respond by growing more connections to process the additional information. The logical explanation would be that stimulating experiences create more robust, complex, and flexible brains. Thus, a stimulating and challenging classroom will optimize plasticity, brain growth, and learning.

The Allure of the Unknown

If a child is to keep alive his inborn sense of wonder, he needs the companionship of at least one adult who can share it, rediscovering with him the joy, excitement, and mystery of the world we live in.

Rachel Carson

Some of us like nothing better than to jump out of airplanes or to get lost in unfamiliar lands. Others are happy to stay close to home and do the same thing every day. How we experience novelty depends on whether we find it rewarding or anxiety provoking. Each of us thrives at a different level of challenge and risk. Not surprisingly, the brain networks that regulate exploratory behavior connect to those that allow us to learn. This is rooted in our evolutionary history, where survival favored those tribes that had at least a few members who felt the compulsion to see what lay beyond the horizon.

Orienting toward unfamiliar sights and sounds starts in the first few days of life. By four months, infants begin to prefer unexpected sounds over familiar ones, with a similar shift for visual objects between seven and eleven months. For most children and adolescents, social investigation is preferred to environmental exploration and, as you might have predicted, girls show a greater preference for social investigation than boys.

Novelty and Learning

- Attraction to novelty occurs spontaneously in most mammals.
- Novelty activates the biochemistry and neuroplasticity of learning.
- Novelty stimulates information processing, memory, and learning.

Novelty and Attachment

- Novelty triggers positive social behavior that reduces stress and increases exploration.
- Separation from parents results in less mobility and exploratory behavior.
- Comfort with novelty correlates with less anxiety and social engagement.

Anxiety and fear are enemies of curiosity and exploration. Traumatized people often develop what is called neophobia—the fear of anything new. Inhibited and anxious children tend to grow into adults who avoid exploration and novelty. If the classroom has been a place of consistent failure, shutting down may be a student's only defense against the anticipated fear, shame, and humiliation. Anxious and traumatized students also find it difficult to use their imagination, engage in role-play, or discuss hypothetical situations. They just generate too much uncertainty. This aspect of neophobia affects their performance in the classroom.

While throwing some beginners into the deep end of a pool will teach them to swim, others become frightened enough never to learn at all. It is with these students that emotional nurturance is most important. The brain needs to be in a mild to moderate state of arousal for learning to take place. Because anxiety and learning are so closely interwoven, a teacher's ability to take a child's "emotional temperature" and regulate his or her anxiety are vital ingredients of success. Introducing play can also facilitate learning in all students and may be especially helpful for more anxious students.

Play

Games lubricate the body and the mind.

Benjamin Franklin

What does play have to do with learning? The development of the brain is based on the stimulation of the body and the senses in interaction with the world and other people. Thus, play is pure learning, although little formal study has been dedicated to the relationship of play to learning, it is obvious that play can be used as both a motivational and teaching tool.

On the surface, humans and other animals play because it's fun, but our instincts drive us to play because of its role in building skills required for adaptation and survival. Here are some examples: seagulls purposely drop and catch objects, simulating hunting skills, while dolphins practice swimming accuracy by creating rings of bubbles to swim through. Many social animals, including humans, engage in rough-and-tumble play to test their strength and establish social hierarchies.

From the early months of life, a game of peek-a-boo brings joy to both children and adults by stimulating the biochemistry of reward and well-being. These early experiences serve to associate play with social connectivity, warm feelings, and a sense of accomplishment. A few years later, play among boys and girls serves as rehearsal for more mature courtship and mating behavior. Throughout life, playful actions are experienced as expressions of positive feelings, safety, and togetherness.

The Effects of Play

- Play stimulates feelings of joy and well-being (via endorphins, dopamine, and serotonin).
- Rough-and-tumble play is regulated by levels of testosterone and adrenaline.
- Rough-and-tumble play enhances learning (via gene expression and neural growth in the brain).

With the emergence of language in humans, play emerged in word games, debate, arguments, and friendly verbal banter. All of this verbal play strengthens the organization of mental structures while sustaining interest and excitement about remembering and learning. Although imaginative behavior seems disconnected from physical activity, the two are inextricably interwoven. We know that imagining behavior helps subsequent performance through internal practice. Games like hide and seek tap into hunting instincts related to tracking and foraging while Simon Says improves inhibitory motor control and executive abilities. Overall, play provides learning experiences that result in expanded skills and abilities for classroom learning.

Play and Social Learning

The clearest way into the Universe is through a forest wilderness.

John Muir

Social animals engage in a variety of play fighting generally referred to as rough-and-tumble play, which builds the strength, stamina, and skills needed for hunting and protection while enhancing turn taking, sharing, and a sense of fairness. Simultaneously, the positive emotions generated during such play inhibit aggression against the kin you will need on your side in real battles. The exaggerated moves, fakes, and attempts at deception may all be related to predicting, anticipating, and avoiding the behaviors of potential enemies. Football, rugby, and many other sports are direct descendants of these primitive activities.

I am certainly not the first to suggest that sports are a form of civilized combat with bats and balls substituted for spears and swords. The same mental and social skills required for survival during most of our evolutionary history are all employed in sports. Perhaps this is why guys who play ball on the weekends are called weekend warriors and why teams are said to battle, fight it out, and clash with one another. Not so coincidentally, I first learned how to calculate averages and percentages by figuring out baseball statistics in elementary school, making my interest in sports a motivational tool for skills in other areas of learning.

Play fighting helps establish a dominance hierarchy in a controlled manner while regulating aggression and encouraging social communication. I received a lesson in establishing dominance many years ago when I spent a week with an Alaskan wolf. It was clear that he was not just a big dog—this wolf was stronger, more agile, and of higher intelligence than any dog I had ever encountered. One day, as we parked our truck, the wolf jumped out and was greeted by a dog of about the same size.

Within seconds they took off at full speed in the direction of a large hedge. When they got to the hedge, the dog crashed into the bushes while the wolf gracefully sprang over them onto the far wall. The dog, composing itself, shot once again across the courtyard with the wolf in pursuit. In no time, the wolf was on the dog's tail, tripping him into a rolling cloud of dust. The dog jumped up, shook off the dust, and both of them headed straight for us. They arrived simultaneously, and the dog immediately rolled on its back and bared its neck. We had witnessed the establishment of the dominance hierarchy of a new pack in about half a minute. They could now cooperate and get along, clearly knowing who was the boss.

Thus, the existing cultural separation between education and play is contradicted by research that shows play enhances sensory-motor and social-emotional development, abstract thinking, problem solving, and academic achievement. Evolution has shaped our brains to engage with the world in ways that support our gender-based social roles. In other words, our brains have evolved to attend to and learn those things that are personally, socially, and ecologically relevant. You may have noticed that you almost never have to bribe children to play video games or use social media. These modern contrivances are so compelling because they tap into genetically programmed and biologically reinforced instincts. Could the best way to teach be to package learning as play? Is this one of the secrets of the video game industry that educators refuse to believe?

Application Box: Dropping Eggs and Building Teams

A central goal of a tribe and its culture is to support survival by consistently improving problem-solving capabilities. Group problem solving stimulates traditional tribal interactions and teaches all of the individuals about the capacities and skills of their fellow tribe members. If you haven't already heard about it, you can utilize a helpful exercise called the great egg drop. The group must figure out how to create a package for an egg that will allow it to be dropped 8 feet without breaking. This involves discussion, research, exploring the environment for potentially useful materials, and many rounds of research and development. The great egg drop is also fun because failure makes a mess.

A project like this can serve as a practice run for other, more significant problems that the class might want to tackle next. The next challenge for the group may be to find a solution related to a worthy cause that the group has already identified. Your students can use the same group processes that they used for the great egg drop to explore solutions. Kids may also be interested in how other kids have found solutions to problems in their communities. This can be explored through a teacher-guided Internet or library search.

The world is full of team-building exercises because so many teachers, coaches, and business leaders realize the importance of establishing securely attached groups to maximize learning and productivity. These activities provide work-arounds within groups in modern industrial situations and activate primitive social instincts. Don't be afraid to look for materials from the fields of business management and leadership; although you may have to modify the exercises a bit, the principles are exactly the same as they are in classroom.

The Acting and Reacting Brain

There is more wisdom in your body than in your deepest philosophy.
                                        Friedrich Nietzsche

We live in a three-dimensional world embedded in the flow of time. Networks in the frontal lobes of the brain have developed to organize our sense of time. The parietal lobes, which are located on the sides of our brains, create the ability for us to experience our bodies and the space around us. Together, the frontal and parietal lobes, along with scores of other neural systems, construct our experience of space and time. This allows us to navigate our physical and social worlds. It is in the context of space-time that all of our experience and learning occurs.

Within this inner world, we can imagine ourselves, experiment with alternative perspectives and emotions, and rehearse for behaviors in the external world. Without the ability to reflect on our reactions, imagine alternatives, and sometimes cancel reflexive physical and emotional responses, there is little freedom from being a biological machine reacting to the environment. The implications for education include an understanding of the sensory-motor contribution to conceptual and abstract learning and the importance of physical activity and play.

Application Box

Take advantage of creative activities that call on students to express themselves and share these expressions with the class. Have them create narratives, musical compositions, or works of art that embody personal experiences and shared visions. You may want to create a class mural, totem, or sculpture that contains and combines expressions from each student. The work of art can become a pictorial representation of the individual and combined identities of the group.

The curricular focus on concepts and abstract information makes it easy to discount the role of the body in learning. Yet the biology of all learning is grounded in the navigation of physical space. This may be why the hippocampus, which serves as a cognitive map of the environment in mammals, is also the portal to all conceptual learning in humans. Additionally, this could be why using the large muscles in our legs triggers the release of neural growth hormones that turbocharge memory and learning. In essence, our muscles have evolved to tell the brain to pay attention and learn when we are in motion. The physical activity involved in play helps students learn. Engaging your students in physical activity will help them remember your lessons and encourage participation.

Another central aspect of living is navigating our many interpersonal relationships. The sensory, motor, and spatial components of our attachment systems become interwoven with our experience of self, others, and the physical environment. Think for a moment about how we describe our interpersonal emotions—we fall in love, fly into a rage, or have a hard time handling what a loved one has just told us. Even the words *bonding* and *attachment* evoke an image of joining together two separate objects in space. Attachment schemas are not abstract concepts; they are stored in implicit memory and manifest in our musculature, posture, gait, and interpersonal stance. People can tell us they love us, but they have to show us with actions.

Imagine sitting with a new friend and his three-year-old son, paying special attention to their many interactions. When we first enter the house, the child holds his father's leg, leans into it, and rolls around the back so as to watch us from a safe vantage point. A little later he presents his finger, which he has pinched in the door of a toy car, for his father to kiss. At another point, he sneaks up from behind with a pillow and hits his father on the head as an introduction to some rough-and-tumble play. Still later, he finishes his juice box and hands it to his father with the words "all done." These interactions demonstrate the boy's ability to successfully use his father for safety, solace, stimulation, and service.

Based on these experiences, this child will likely enter school with the expectation of similar positive and useful connections with his teacher. He may assume that the teacher will also be a source of safety, solace, stimulation, and service; he may be able to learn strategies for the classroom such as raising his hand, sharing with his classmates, and approaching his teacher for comfort. This relaxed and open state of mind minimizes anxiety while maximizing neural plasticity and learning in the student, which then promotes enthusiasm in the teacher.

The opposite would be the anxious or traumatized learner who sees the teacher as a threat and lacks the skills to grasp the materials placed in front of him. This may be caused by trauma at home or previous negative experiences with teachers. Such children may appear withdrawn, or they may exhibit defensive postures. Some children enter school without many of the skills required to successfully utilize teachers and classrooms. In many instances, students first need to be taught how to learn before engaging with the material to be learned.

When children have positive and rewarding experiences with parents and other authority figures, they are more likely to be able to use the teacher as a source of emotional regulation and learning. This can be reflected through a relaxed body, leaning toward the teacher when something interests them, curiosity, and an optimistic attitude about being successful learners.

Turning Students into Stars

The voyage of discovery is not in seeking new landscapes but in having new eyes.

Marcel Proust

Over the course of his long career, actor turned elementary school teacher Albert Cullum wove his love of acting and his love of teaching into a vital and lively classroom experience. As a teacher in a middle-class suburb, he did not face the challenges of poverty or community violence. As he saw it, his enemies were complacency, mediocrity, and a blind acceptance of the status quo. He faced these challenges by making education a sensory, motor, and emotional challenge through the power of his personality and the skills he learned while on stage.

Early on, Cullum realized that when play becomes the culture of the classroom, disciplinary problems decrease while learning increases. He felt that it was the nature of children to learn through active and imaginative play, which in turn stimulated enthusiasm, imagination, and openness to new ideas. He structured all of his learning activities to channel his students' youthful energy toward productive ends.

Cullum's use of plays to teach in elementary school was something that many of his colleagues believed to be impossible. He used the works of Shakespeare and Shaw as vehicles to teach language, history, and human values, while encouraging self-expression and personal transformation. In an era characterized by Dick and Jane, Cullum opted for Romeo and Juliet, Macbeth, and Lear. By presenting his students with highly challenging content, he communicated a message of confidence in their intelligence, maturity, and capabilities. Cullum found that when he presented even his youngest students with a worthy challenge, they rose to the occasion, bonded more closely with one another, and gained self-confidence.

He believed that by playing these heroic roles, young children found themselves fighting for bigger things in life. The process is bound to build self-esteem. The physicality of acting allowed children to learn the lessons of each play not only through words, but also in their bodies, minds, and hearts. The engagement with the material via performance led to an embodiment of knowledge and made each student a hero by being a cast member of a timeless story.

Cullum's classroom was always filled with the kind of noise you hear at a birthday party—children playing, laughing, moving, and touching everything around them. He created a learning environment that activated both explicit and implicit memory systems by blending history, art, music, literature, and math into fun, tactile, and emotionally engaging activities. Mr. Cullum was always in the middle of the fun. Never quite getting over being an actor, he would teach about the geography of Canada and Alaska while wearing a bear costume—his lessons were never dull or passive experiences. When they weren't swimming down the Mississippi River that they created out of construction paper that flowed through the classroom, students were competing in the math Olympics, geography races, or art shows.

Cullum assumed that a sense of safety and belonging were essential elements of successful education. He endeavored to communicate love, compassion, and respect to his students, which he saw carried into their relationships with one another. The bonds established transcended age, race, and status. As the sole African American student in Cullum's class stated at a reunion decades later, "I felt as though my classmates loved me. I felt as though my teacher loved me." As an expression of Cullum's caring, he established a democratic classroom environment to maximize a sense of investment and pride in being a member of the group.

Into his later years, Cullum retained the rare ability to see the world through the eyes of a child. As a teacher of teachers at Boston University, he engaged his students in ways that helped to remind them of the world of children. He believed that in order to become a good teacher, one had to rediscover the child within. In order to transform what he described as the "cancer of mediocrity" that he saw undermining his profession, Cullum believed that teacher training should include guided self-development.

Much of Cullum's success lay in his ability to give voice to the perspective of children, his sense of accountability for his students' education, and his revolutionary curricula and teaching methods. By becoming fully engaged in the way children learn—through movement, emotions, activities, and play—he felt that teachers can open the floodgates to learning. While initially drawn to the classroom to be a star, his goal became to make a star of each of his students.

How can we channel the spirit of Albert Cullum in our classrooms? The first step may be to reimagine how we teach to include more physical interaction with the curriculum. For example, Cullum's lesson on the Mississippi River included drawing a map of the United States in the parking lot and making a river out of butcher paper that students could swim down from Minnesota to New Orleans. The second step may be to reflect upon how we might underestimate what our students are capable of and push them a bit further with bigger issues and more complex challenges. Finally, we can look into our hearts to see if there are ways we are withholding our full commitment to our students. If, upon reflection, we find out that we are holding back, we can take risks to be more present, more vulnerable, and more invested in our attachment to them.

Exercise 8:
Into the Unknown

Experiment with the unexpected. While our brains are equipped for novelty, it is easy for humans to fall into habits of thinking, feeling, and behaving that result in avoiding new experiences. Neophobia (the fear of anything new) can be all the more prevalent for those who are anxious or who have had frightening experiences. As a general rule, I would encourage you to build the unexpected into your classroom practices in ways that match the age and abilities of your students. It is important not to overwhelm, but it just as important not to underwhelm. While field trips are great for exposure to the unfamiliar, we don't need anything big or dramatic to experience novelty. Here are a few suggestions of new ways of experiencing the everyday that can be done for free in the classroom.

Combining exposure to novelty with physical movement seems to create a positive synergy of body and mind, leading to a sense of confidence in the face of the unknown. One of my favorite exercises is a blindfolded exploration of the classroom. Five students at a time can be blindfolded and allowed to explore any safe physical space while the other students silently look on. The teacher can ask each student in turn to describe what he or she is sensing and feeling. Nonblindfolded students can be placed around the room where there are sharp edges or other potential dangers and can be instructed to gently guide the blindfolded students away from them. Students can also be provided with sticks that they can slide across the floor in front of them to detect furniture and other obstacles.

Students can be encouraged to pay closer attention to their other senses to see if they become heightened or if they provide clues as to their location or the presence of others. You can ask them questions such as:

- What does it feel like to be blindfolded and watched by others? Scary? Vulnerable? Peaceful?
- What would it be like to have to get back and forth to school blindfolded?
- What might it be like to be blind?

If it is possible to make your classroom dark enough, you may want to try having all of the students sit at their desks in the darkness and pay attention to their other senses. A common mindfulness exercise is to encourage everyone to get into a calm and peaceful state of mind and body as they sit at their desks. The next step is to very slowly eat a raisin, M&M, or some other small food left on their desks. Instruct students to pay attention to the sensations related to letting it melt in their mouths and slowly make its way down their throats. Come to think of it, this may be an interesting way to eat lunch together from time to time.

CHAPTER 9

Storytelling:
The First Classroom

No, no! The adventures first, explanations take such a dreadful time.

Lewis Carroll

O̲ur social brains evolved within oral traditions that relied upon storytelling to store learning and wisdom, and transmit tribal culture from generation to generation. Due to the historical importance of stories, we are much better at remembering them than separate pieces of information. In addition, stories play a role in emotional regulation and group connectedness, as well as serving as templates of behavior. Storytellers have been teachers since prehistory—gathering to listen to stories was the first classroom. Teaching through stories instead of lists of facts is a true tribal work-around that leverages the brain's natural abilities in the service of learning.

Imagine a first grade teacher, sitting on the floor surrounded by his students, reading a story about Oliver the elephant. Oliver is one of eleven elephants delivered to a circus that only needs ten, so he is turned away and left to make it on his own. Although rejected again and again, he remains optimistic and in remarkably good elephant spirits. Eventually, Oliver is spotted dancing with some children by the circus master who originally turned him away. Of course, a dancing elephant is just what the circus needs, and Oliver is reunited with his ten friends and given a home. That is the surface story, very much like the ones that wise elders have been telling for 10,000 years (Hoff, 2000).

Now imagine turning around and looking at the faces of the children as they strain to see the pictures in the book. When Oliver is turned away from the circus, brows furrow and uncomfortable expressions fill the room; the children discover their own fears and concerns in Oliver's dilemma. "They just sent him away? Where are his parents? What is he going to eat?" Feeling confused and disoriented is a common experience for young children, and abandonment is their greatest fear. What a relief when Oliver is back with his old friends and appreciated for his true self—an elephant that loves to dance.

Traveling with Oliver on a vicarious journey within the context of a safe and loving classroom allows all of the children to feel and think about their fears of rejection and abandonment. The fact that the hero of this story is an elephant allows these terrifying feelings to be explored at a safe distance. Look again. Near the back of the room, a little girl named Sophie has tears in her eyes. Her teacher has been concerned with her recent lack of progress, but he is unable to get in touch with her parents to set up a conference. She is very private, so he doesn't bring attention to her by asking if something is wrong during class.

At the end of the day, the teacher asks how Sophie liked Oliver's story. Sophie says that she liked it very much, but that it made her sad. "Why?" asked her teacher. "Because I think Oliver felt the way I feel at night when my mom gets drunk and I can't wake her up. I just stare at her and don't know what to do. Oliver must have felt terrible." Through the story, the teacher discovers that the quiet girl in the back of his classroom is a little hero fighting for her soul. A door swings open to a deeper and more meaningful connection between them and presents the opportunity for Sophie to form a deeper attachment with her teacher.

Stories Are Essential

If history were taught in the form of stories, it would never be forgotten.

Rudyard Kipling

For countless generations, humans have gathered to share stories. Be it tales of their ancestors, strategies for a successful hunt, or to pass the time with friends and family, the stories of a tribe serve as a repository of shared knowledge, emotional stability, and group coherence. Stories connect us, shape our identities, and serve the development, integration, and regulation of our brains.

The central role of storytelling in contemporary tribes attests to its early origins and its central role in memory storage, emotional regulation, and social cohesion. It is very likely that our brains have evolved to be as complex as they are because of the capacity of stories to power imagination. Through the profound transformations from oral, to written, to digital-based record keeping, we have never lost our interest in stories, especially about each other. Just think of all the energy we invest in gossiping through every medium of communication.

Application Box

Gathering to tell and listen to stories is the evolutionary precursor to the modern classroom. Our brains and our cultures have coevolved with storytelling, the structure of narratives, and the tale of heroes. Always use stories when you teach, no matter the age of your students. And when you choose the stories, make sure that they focus on human relationships, integrity, and overcoming challenges. These stories and the messages they contain will infect the minds of the members of your tribe, bringing them closer together and enhancing their ability to learn.

The stories we tell about ourselves are co-constructed with parents and peers and become powerful tools in the creation and maintenance of a sense of self that serves to perpetuate both healthy and unhealthy aspects of self-identity. Positive self-narratives aid in emotional security and minimize the need for elaborate psychological defenses, while negative self-narratives promote pessimism, low self-esteem, and decreases in exploration and learning. By rewriting negative self-narratives, teachers can buffer students from stress while better preparing them to learn.

Stories, Learning, and the Oral Tradition

I do not know whether there are gods, but there ought to be.

Diogenes

Every culture has myths and fables born long before the written word that were passed down via storytelling and song. Before writing, the accumulation and advancement of knowledge was completely dependent on our compulsion to hear and tell stories and the brain's ability to remember them. This is probably why our brains struggle to remember facts while having a limitless storage capacity for stories and songs. Memory experts use this evolutionary legacy to recall large amounts of unconnected information by placing them in a narrative.

They may picture a room and place each of the items they are trying to remember in a different location. For recall, they go back to the visual image of the room and visualize each individual item where they placed it. This is not superhuman; they have simply learned to use the deep well of contextual and narrative memory we all share.

I am a terrible speller and have trouble with the simplest words. I can, however, spell "Mississippi" and "encyclopedia" because when I was young, Disney cartoons spelled these words in songs. And I doubt that anyone from my generation can spell "respect" without hearing Aretha Franklin's voice in our heads. It is also true that most of us can hear the first few notes of thousands of songs we learned years ago and almost immediately be able to sing along. The words and notes seem to be waiting in our brains even though it may be decades since we last heard them. These are all contemporary holdovers of our brains' historic dependence on story and song to hold our memories. Using stories and songs as educational work-arounds in the classroom facilitates learning at all ages.

Another window to our deep history is in the way elders and children relate to stories. It has always been the job of the tribal elders to tell stories, passing them on to the younger members of the tribe. Most of us have elderly relatives who tell the same stories about the past again and again as if we have never heard them before. Now think of who likes to hear the same stories again and again and again in exactly the same way. If you guessed young children, you are right. Children demand that you tell them the same story every night for days, weeks, or months before they are ready to move on to the next one. What we are witnessing in both young and old is a genetically programmed impulse to repeatedly tell and listen to stories for the purpose of transferring culture from generation to generation.

Although stories appear imprecise and unscientific, they serve as powerful organizing tools for neural network integration. Consider this: the structure of any story contains two basic elements. The first is a series of events grounded in the passage of time, and the second is some emotional challenge that gives the story meaning. In order to tell a good story, the language centers of the left hemisphere must integrate with the centers in the right hemisphere that process emotional, sensory-motor, and visual information.

A story well told provides the brain with the best template and strategy for the organization of thinking across the two hemispheres. In fact, the coherence and understandability of the personal narratives we generate are highly related to the security of our attachment relationships, self-esteem, and emotional regulation. In the classroom, narratives serve as a powerful memory tool and a blueprint for behavior and self-identity. Because narratives require the participation of multiple memory networks, stories can enhance memory by storing information across multiple regions of the brain.

A learner's self-narrative, either good or bad, becomes a blueprint for thoughts, feelings, and behaviors that turn into self-fulfilling prophecies. Students with traumatic learning histories incorporate the negative evaluations of parents, teachers, guidance counselors, and other students into their self-references. When negative statements become part of the learner's self-narrative, they raise stress and diminish success. On the other hand, personal narratives of success reduce anxiety and enhance neuroplasticity. Editing negative self-narratives can be a central component of making a challenged learner into a successful student.

A good indicator of the power of stories is reflected in the faces of the listeners. Have you ever noticed what happens to students when you transition from talking about facts and ideas to telling a story? Eye contact locks in, distractions decrease, and a series of expressions reflect the events and emotions that run through the story. You can see the unfolding drama reflected in their eyes, on their faces, and in their bodies. When we look into the eyes of our students while they are immersed in stories, we are seeing the reflections of an ancient campfire that still burns within all of us. Sitting in a circle sharing stories has been a means of human connection and learning back into prehistory. It is a way to tap into primitive social instincts that make us lean into one another, feel connected, and deepen the bonds that weave a group of individuals into a tribe.

Emotional Regulation

I'm not afraid of storms, for I am learning to sail my ship.
Louisa May Alcott

During the first eighteen months of life, the brain's right hemisphere experiences a sensitive period of development as the physical and emotional aspects of interpersonal experience begin to take shape. As the left hemisphere enters its sensitive period during the middle of the second year, spoken language begins to slowly take shape and integrate with the emotional aspects of communication already organized in the right hemisphere. By four to five years, the brain has matured to the point where words and feelings can begin to be linked in meaningful ways. Putting feelings into words and placing them in the context of ongoing experience gradually turns into the ability to regulate our emotions.

Writing about experiences in diaries and journals also supports emotional regulation. Journaling about personally important emotional conflicts results in a cascade of positive biological and emotional effects. For example, journaling has been shown to result in reduced physical symptoms, physician visits, and work absenteeism. Teachers may find it helpful to have each student keep a journal. You can even dedicate ten minutes a day to writing in it.

Having a story helps us remember where we have come from, where we are, and where we are going. This blueprint helps us to avoid feeling lost or overwhelmed by the present while reducing the anxiety and stress of uncertainty. Putting feelings into words and sharing them with others is a learned ability that is based on the skills and encouragement of others. Parents who lack this ability or don't talk to their children about feelings deprive them of a valuable source of emotional regulation. For these children, a teacher may be the first adult in their lives with this capacity.

Application Box

At some point at every grade level, students should be encouraged to write their story in three acts. The first act is a description of what has made them who they are today. The second act should focus on their present interests, the challenges they face, and the concerns they are struggling with. The third act should focus on how they plan to master their present challenges and what they see as their next challenge on the horizon. Each of the three acts should contain three levels of description—their actions in the world, their inner emotional experience, and their reflection and understanding of what is happening inside of them. The articulation of these dimensions correlates with both secure attachment and resilience.

The next assignment is to have the class co-construct a narrative of their year together using the same format. Start by taking stock of where the class is today in the categories of accomplishments and strengths. Next, have the class target short-, medium-, and long-term goals for the academic year. These goals should be in a few categories such as character, academics, community service, and so on. The third part is to write the story of how these goals will be accomplished, including the results and detailed plans for a celebration that will held at the end of the school year. This assignment serves multiple purposes including creating a shared vision, improving buy-in, enhancing group collaboration, and creating a blueprint in everyone's imagination about how the year will go as everyone progresses toward success.

Secure Attachment and Integrated Narratives

Educational policies are passed that don't make sense, and we teach anyway.

Rita Pierson

Narratives begin to be co-constructed in parent-child talk early in a child's life. This process continues at school with teachers, peers, and in an ever-broadening array of social situations throughout life. When verbal interactions include references to feelings, behaviors, and knowledge, they provide a medium to integrate inner and outer experience in a coherent manner.

From primitive tribes to modern classrooms, the participation of caretakers, teachers, and children in narrating shared experiences organizes memories and ties us together. When caretakers are unable to tolerate certain emotions, these emotions will be excluded from their narratives or shaped into distorted but more acceptable forms. Whatever is excluded from the narrative will be more difficult for children to process and comprehend in the years to come. At the extreme, parents can be so overwhelmed by unresolved trauma that their narratives become disjointed and incoherent. This will be reflected in the way their children describe their own experiences. Oftentimes, teachers are in a position to help students edit their personal narratives that have been shaped by trauma and loss. By being positive and by expecting greatness from students, teachers can help reshape negative narratives.

Securely attached children generally engage in self-talk during toddlerhood and more spontaneous self-reflective remarks by age six. They tend to make comments about their thinking processes and their ability to remember things about their history. As you might expect, children who are abused are usually insecurely attached and less able to engage in self-reflection. When parents are unable to verbalize their inner experiences, their children's capacity to use language to organize and integrate conscious experience is left undeveloped. Their options are to express their feelings through acting out or convert them into physical symptoms.

If a child is able to achieve this ability with the help of someone other than the primary caretaker, like a teacher, he or she may be able to earn a higher level of security and integration. This help can come from teachers who attune well to their students and assist in the articulation of their emotional life. All of this strongly suggests that teachers who can respect children's vulnerability while helping them to verbalize their thoughts and feelings can increase children's ability to regulate their anxiety and build a positive self-identity.

The Heroic Journey

Wisdom outweighs any wealth.

Sophocles

Every *heroic journey* needs a hero with whom the audience can identify. Next, every hero needs two challenges: (1) an external challenge (the dragon), and (2) an inner wound (parental rejection or past failure) that causes deep and persistent emotional pain. Through the first two acts, the hero fails to meet the challenge or avoids it altogether and struggles with doubt about having what it takes to succeed. The challenge is repeatedly resisted, questioned, and even rejected before it is eventually accepted. During the journey, the hero leaves behind old definitions of self before discovering personal meaning and a new identity. Some inner transformation takes place that allows him or her to face the challenge and succeed.

> The *heroic journey*, or myth of the hero, is a basic narrative that appears in storytelling around the world. The structure of the hero's journey appears to reflect the inner transition from adolescence to adulthood, the forging of personal identity, and the development of behaviors and values that support the survival and well-being of the tribe.

This narrative structure, seen in stories around the world and throughout time, has been called the myth of the hero (Campbell, 1968). It is the basic theme of ancient mythology, contemporary literature, and most children's stories. It is the adolescent struggle toward adulthood, the overcoming of fear after abandonment and trauma, and the striving for personal transformation and redemption. The universality of this story is likely the result of the commonality of brain evolution, shared developmental challenges, and the fundamental emotional challenges of human experience. Despite our cultural differences, all humans share the struggle to be successful in love and work.

Central Aspects of the Hero's Journey

The Journey Begins

The hero has an outer challenge to be faced and an inner brokenness to be healed.

Accomplishing these goals requires taking a journey to new and unknown places.

The journey offers a promise of growth and redemption.

Finding the Guide

The guide acknowledges and respects the brokenness and shame that lurk in the hero's shadow.

The guide sees beyond the hero's limitations.

The guide presents an invitation and a challenge to take the heroic journey.

Attaching to the Guide

The guide has something and believes the hero can have it too.

The hero becomes aware that the guide sees something real in the world and in the hero.

The hero comes to gradually share the guide's vision.

The Challenge

The present system and the current self are insufficient and cannot save the hero.

One must venture forth beyond the safe and familiar confines of one's life and beliefs.

Past rules will be broken in the cause of finding what can only be found elsewhere.

The Heroic Discovery

Limitations exist only in the mind.

Confronting fear and pain opens gateways to new worlds.

Power is discovered in vulnerability; freedom is found in commitment.

Children who come to be designated as unteachable are usually fighting a heroic battle for survival. Although the causes of their external challenges may range from poverty and abuse to neglect by overly privileged parents, their internal pain almost always stems from experiences of abandonment and shame. These children need to be guided by a wise elder, a teacher that is capable of being emotionally nurturing and intellectually challenging in equal parts. Within secure attachment relationships, articulating and sharing their journey creates a bridge to those around them. The universality of struggle allows students to connect with their peers. Understanding their own story also allows for a more objective perspective on their internal struggles as well as input from others.

Carl Jung said that the answers to our most important questions are to be found in the shadow. The shadow is the repository of our pain, shame, and the demons of our inner lives. Because you can't completely banish the shadow, you must learn to develop a relationship with it. If the shadow can be acknowledged and included as part of the emotional reality of the classroom, the teacher becomes transformed from a source of information to a guide on the path to *wisdom*.

> ***Wisdom*** is the sharing of knowledge and experience, offered with compassion, and presented in a manner that helps others to heal and grow. Wisdom is knowledge in service to others.

Everyone has a story. In the absence of self-awareness or the ability to reflect on our own thinking, our story is a simple chronology of the events of our life and the judgments we have about them. Teaching a higher vantage point adds self-awareness and an objective distance that provides us with the ability to think about our story, reflect on our choices, and consider editing the outcomes. Sometimes you have to make some suggestions about alternative narrative arcs and outcomes to get students started. If I focus on my work and study hard, could I get good grades? Could I graduate from high school, go to college, and get a good job? What if the suffering in my life has meaning?

The heroic teacher acknowledges the suffering, hypocrisy, and lack of fairness in the world and makes it a part of the classroom experience. The teacher then invites the students to take a journey into a world beyond the limitations of their current perspectives.

Like the shaman, teachers need to have a clear vision of their mission so that their students can come to believe that teachers see something real that is worth working for. The guide's message must be, "I know something you don't know, something you don't have, but I am committed to sharing it with you and bringing you on this journey." Teachers tell stories of what is possible that become the blueprint for the heroic journey.

In order for teachers to become guides for their students' journeys, they must first articulate their own journey and become familiar with their own broken places. Increasing mindfulness and courage in the face of personal challenges and fears will allow teachers to become the heroes of their own stories as a guide to others. Because teachers who create or adhere to unfair rules will be seen as too insecure and frightened to be a guide, heroic teachers must be brave enough to break the rules in the service of their students. A demoralized or burned-out teacher cannot be a positive guide or a model of heroism.

The narrative process allows us to separate story from self. It's like taking off your shirt to patch a tear and then putting it back on. When we evolved the capacity to examine our narratives and see them as one option among many, we also gained the ability to edit and modify our lives (White, 2007). Teachers hope to guide their students to the realization that they are more than characters in a story dictated by external circumstance. We would love to instill in our students the knowledge that they can make choices, follow their passions, and become the author of a new story—their story. The remarkable heroic journey of a teacher and her students is embodied in the work of high school teacher Erin Gruwell (2007; Freedom Writers with Gruwell, 2007).

Erin Gruwell

The whole problem with the world is that fools and fanatics are always so certain of themselves, and wiser people so full of doubts.

Bertrand Russell

Erin Gruwell came to Wilson High School in Long Beach, California, as a student teacher from upscale Newport Beach. While only 30 miles separate Newport and Long Beach, they are worlds apart. Wilson's reputation as one of the most culturally diverse high schools in the country initially drew Gruwell there. However, she soon learned that what had been labeled as "integration" consisted of separate and hostile ethnic groups and that the desks and books in her classroom were falling apart and etched with gang symbols.

Her students had been labeled by other teachers as learning disabled, behaviorally challenged, and unteachable. It turned out that she had been assigned all of the students no one else wanted to teach and soon realized that they had more serious things to worry about than literature and history. She discovered that some students were traumatized by beatings from their stepfathers or they were grieving the loss of friends killed by gang violence. One of her students told her, "When you have nothing to live for, you look for reasons to die." She soon came to realize her students needed to be healed before they would be able to learn, so she decided to turn to stories.

Gruwell wanted to give her students a way to share their own stories, so she gave them journals to write about their lives, their problems at home, the deaths of friends and family members to gang violence, and their encounters with racism. She shaped her lesson plans to show her students a way out of violence by teaching them to tell their stories. This proved to be her most successful tool—a way for her students to express themselves, be heard, and learn how to better listen to each other. She slowly became aware that they were healing through writing.

A key to Gruwell's teaching style is to connect her students' vulnerabilities and passions to relevant and realistic stories about tagging, living in the projects, and being incarcerated. She enticed them with questions like, What would happen if a Latina and an African American hooked up as a parallel to Romeo and Juliet. Later, Gruwell took a leap to create lessons that ignite a desire to go beyond the walls of the classroom.

She recounts a particularly teachable moment when a student had drawn a caricature of another student, depicting him as having abnormally large lips. The note made its way around the classroom and eventually to the student it portrayed. The drawing reminded her of propaganda she had seen from Nazi-era Germany, when Jews were depicted as rats with long noses. With a fire inside she hadn't felt before, she grabbed the note, raised her hand in the air, and asked her students who had heard of the Holocaust. To her surprise, only a few students had, and this is where her tribe's journey truly began.

It was then that she understood that her job was not only to teach her students English, but also to educate them about history, racism, and injustice. She took her class to the Museum of Tolerance. She found that they were able to relate to the pain and suffering of the Jews: being afraid to go outside their neighborhood, feeling ostracized from society, and fighting to overcome adversity. They wrote to Miep Gies (the woman who hid Anne Frank and her family) and Zlata Filipovic (2006; a teenage author who wrote *Zlata's Diary: A Child's Life in Sarajevo*) and, not deterred by cost or logistics, invited them to come to speak to the class. Not surprisingly, they were well received.

Gruwell acted as a matriarchal tribal chief who was bold enough to approach people in power to open doors for her students. She endured alienation, gossip, and criticism from her peers while staying true to her commitment to her students. One of her biggest accomplishments was to get the school administration to allow her to continue teaching the same group of students for two additional years, a powerful acknowledgment that she had been able to create a strong tribe that allowed her to teach the unteachable. She found that as her students shared their pain, the bonds among them overcame the racial barriers that divided them. By expressing their struggles and by being appreciated by their peers, they experienced a shift from feeling indifferent and hopeless to empowered and capable. She showed her students that they could escape their traumatic pasts and positively influence the future and perhaps the world.

After countless journal entries and an ever-deepening appreciation of the power of the written word, they began to call themselves the Freedom Writers, after the freedom riders of the 1960s who rode integrated buses across the South. With Gruwell's encouragement, they compiled their journals into a book, *The Freedom Writers Diary: How a Teacher and 150 Teens Used Writing to Change Themselves and the World Around Them.* The positive reception of the book helped to give meaning to their personal struggles and gave them a way to inspire others to become the heroes of their own stories. During their final year at Wilson, the Freedom Writers received the Spirit of Anne Frank Award for "their commitment to combating discrimination, racism, and bias-related violence" (Freedom Writers with Gruwell, 2007, p. 3).

Gruwell's success demonstrates the profound importance of acknowledging pain and vulnerability to open the door to growth and learning. Consider watching the film about her life and work (*Freedom Writers*) with your class to stimulate discussion about classroom connections and journaling. Making journaling a part of your curriculum will spontaneously address a number of educational goals, making it a very efficient teaching method. The film, along with the journals, may entice your students to engage in a similar project. All teachers have the capacity to help their students rewrite their stories, thereby teaching them that anything is possible.

Exercise 9: Writing Your Own Story

Personal narratives serve the purpose of guiding behavior, providing emotional security, and deepening self-understanding. The ability to identify with the hero of a story provides younger children with positive role models. As they grow older, they are able to internalize these outward representations of strength and courage into aspects of their self-image. In this exercise, students will write their own heroic story.

Act 1: Character Development—Who Were You Then?

Begin with the outline of the aspects of the heroic journey above and translate it to the level of your class. The exercise begins with each student identifying a significant challenge he or she has experienced. For some it may be giving a piano recital, standing up to a bully, or the loss of a loved one. The important consideration is that it is a significant challenge, took courage to face, and was something necessary or worth facing. Once the outer challenge is identified, a key emotion triggered by the challenge needs to be identified, such as sadness, shame, or fear. From these questions you will establish the outer challenge and the inner pain.

Act 2: Inner Growth and Taking on the Challenge— What Did You Do?

The next step is to identify a guide, which can be a person, a set of beliefs, or some part of the self that had to be summoned. Although guides see the challenge and the inner pain, they also see past the hero's limitations and can envision their success. A student might identify a parent, coach, therapist, spiritual figure, or author who helped them to understand their situation and gave them the confidence to move forward. You can ask students to write a bit about the process of how they attached to their guide and came to trust him or her before or during taking up the challenge. Erin Gruwell and other educators described in this book are excellent examples of guides.

The next step is to ask students to discuss and write about what they learned from their guide. It might be that everyone struggles with painful emotions and that you are not alone in your quest. Guides often see our capabilities before we do and hold the vision of our success as we come to recognize it ourselves. One common theme is that your goals in life and the emotions that keep you from going after them are not compatible. If you want to be a concert pianist, you need to take the risk of performing in front of an audience. If you want to hold your head up, you need to confront the bully. If you want to go forward and live your life, you will need to find a way to hold the lost loved one inside yourself and bring the person with you on your quest. These ideas usually violate previous rules and are needed to transform the frightening emotions from an obstacle to a source of motivation.

Act 3: Resolution—Who Are You Now?

The final step is a recognition that limitations of the mind can be objectified and tested, that you can change your mind and behaviors by facing challenges. In fact, confronting fears is the way forward. Freedom, discovery, and fulfillment lie on the other side of facing worthy challenges. The final lesson is that acknowledging and facing fears actually makes us stronger.

The heroic journey is a template for challenges that we face throughout our lives. It is a cyclical process that evolves during development as we reach each new stage of life. It also expands and deepens with each challenge we face and conquer. Everyone can be helped by articulating their story and by being encouraged to move on to the next challenge.

In Chapter 11, I discuss your heroic journey and how it can improve your ability to connect with your students.

PART IV

Tapping Into Primitive Social Instincts

CHAPTER 10

Tribal Work-Arounds
in Practice

A house divided against itself cannot stand.

Abraham Lincoln

*T*hroughout this book, I have presented evidence for the neu-
roplastic power of secure attachments in the context of more natural
learning environments. The basic premise is that the more the environ-
ment of a classroom parallels the interpersonal, emotional, and motiva-
tional components of our tribal past, the more our primitive instincts
will enhance the biochemistry of learning. Further, the benefits of put-
ting your class on a "Paleolithic social diet" through the use of tribal
work-arounds will be most significant with students whose cultural
backgrounds and learning styles are especially mismatched to the mod-
ern industrial classroom. In this chapter, we look at how educators
have used an array of strategies designed to enhance physical safety,
support emotional security, and integrate the values of education into
the broader community. The works of the educators described in this
chapter contain a wealth of ideas about how deepening human connec-
tions strengthen schools and enhance learning.

As a boy, I was one of those troubled and distracted students
who had difficulty learning. Overwhelmed by stress at home
and using most of my energy to cope, I lacked the support,

motivation, and emotional balance to be anything more than a mediocre student. I was, however, fortunate enough to cross paths with a handful of caring teachers with whom I developed strong emotional bonds. In their classes, I somehow found algebra, social studies, and literature interesting and sometimes even inspiring. Tests in these classes became worthy challenges and opportunities to make my teachers proud.

These experiences made it clear to me that loving relationships and secure attachments have the power to heal broken hearts and activate struggling brains. They also instilled within me the subversive idea that I might be capable of earning a living with my head instead of my hands. By the time my tenth grade guidance counselor suggested that I switch from an academic track to an industrial track and my father told me to forget about going to college, I was ready to prove them wrong. I rebelled with a vengeance, staying in school through three graduate degrees.

Application Box

Think of a teacher that had a significant impact on your education. Share this example with your class. Outline the strengths and behaviors that you wish to include in your own teaching style. This will serve as a verbal contract with your students. You can also encourage them to share similar experiences that they had with teachers or other authority figures. You can try to incorporate certain techniques or styles that your students responded to.

Based on my own history, it is easy to see why teachers like Marva Collins and Erin Gruwell are so close to my heart. Perhaps you have a teacher that is close to your heart as well, someone who rebelled against the status quo and discovered more effective ways to teach. It is clear that their success is grounded in the ability to stimulate primitive social instincts through the creation of attachment-based classrooms. If it weren't for teachers like these, many of us would have spent our lives thinking we were unteachable and achieving far less satisfying and productive lives.

As you will see in this chapter, many other heroes are out there fighting the good fight for positive learning through secure attachment. I will share with you brief sketches of three educators—Joe Clark, Jamie Escalante, and Rafe Esquith—to demonstrate how tribal work-arounds have already proven successful.

Physical Safety

I won't say ours was a tough school, but we did have our own coroner.
                                                                Lenny Bruce

Children learn best when they feel connected, appreciated, and safe. The goal of attachment-based teaching is for each child to move from feeling vulnerable, frightened, and unimportant to feeling protected, cared for, and valued. Tribal educators foster an environment of safety by serving as protectors and defenders of their tribe. They promote security through structure, consistency, and keeping a watchful eye for potential danger. The message to each student is, "If any child or adult is bothering you, let me know; I am here to protect you." The prototypical tribal warrior chief is Joe Clark.

Moments before beginning his first day as principal, Clark yelled to the teachers through his bullhorn, "Assume your positions!" In military fashion, the faculty lined up in preparation for the waves of students about to fill the hallways. This was very different from the first day of school a year earlier when a security guard was stabbed for interfering with a drug deal.

Clark was the new sheriff in town, charged with bringing law and order to a few square blocks of Paterson, New Jersey, called Eastside High, a name synonymous with violence, drugs, and academic failure.

Selected for the job based on his past success as principal of a neighboring school, Clark's fundamental belief is that discipline is the essence of education. Clark had zero tolerance for anything that compromised safety or learning. His goals were simple—to support education, to inspire those who wanted to be inspired, and to uplift the school and the community. It was not the stuff of a touchy-feely administrator; educating in a combat zone called for wartime leadership.

In his book *Laying Down the Law,* Clark writes that before his arrival, the students had taken control: "They had the power, they set the tone, and the tone was chaos" (1989, p. 47). He believed that if learning was going to take place, the "diseases of the ghetto" had to be cut out. Before the school year began, Clark had the graffiti covered, new desks installed, and plants, fountains, and couches added to make Eastside look more like a school than a prison. Trophies were taken out of closets, polished, and displayed, and a dress code was implemented so that the students could represent themselves with dignity, self-respect, and professionalism.

He immediately became notorious for expelling students who were wreaking havoc and making it impossible for others to learn. He tossed out the troublemakers, locked the doors, and secured the perimeter to make sure that the students who wanted to learn and the teachers who wanted to educate them were free to get to work. Clark was unwilling to allow a small minority of students to disrupt learning for everyone else.

Clark fired incompetent security guards and replaced them with strong and responsible adults who were dedicated to protecting the school. By circumventing the rules (and in some instances the law) to create a safe learning environment, he risked both his job and his freedom for his students. Doing what he felt was right for his students, at the peril of his own career, is exactly what is expected of a tribal leader, adding to his authority in the eyes of the tribe.

He diligently watched over his students as a surrogate father, walking up to twenty miles a day patrolling the halls and letting everyone know he was on the job. The drug dealers called Clark Batman because he carried a Louisville Slugger when confronting them and getting them to leave the school; others called him Crazy Joe. During his first year as principal, he held back 400 students who were not working up to grade level. In response to the outcry, he replied, "if you think getting left back is hard, try living as an illiterate" (1989, p. 68).

Like any good tribal elder, he also wanted to transmit important cultural values and teach his students to be good citizens, responsible adults, and nurturing parents. To support these goals, he developed extracurricular programs to teach job and life skills. He encouraged teachers to serve as role models because so many of their students had given up on their own parents and had no one else to turn to.

Clark knew that for his students to excel, his teachers needed to feel supported. He promoted teacher pride by encouraging them to ask for what they needed—a fresh coat of paint for their classrooms, new books, whatever would facilitate the learning environment—and he always did his best to deliver what he promised. When teachers went on strike asking for more money, he forbade any teacher from crossing the picket line because he knew they deserved a raise. He made a point of telling his teachers that he didn't blame them for the problems of education, but he did point a finger at fellow principals who were afraid to assume the responsibility of making their schools safe. As Clark sees it, the essential equation for learning is that the student must be able to receive what the teacher is transmitting in the context of peace, order, and mutual respect.

The same principle guiding Clark's attitude and behaviors also applies to classroom teachers. If any of your students is in danger, your first job is to assess the situation, intervene, or get the help you need to keep your students safe. Our students need to know that the adults around them, especially those charged with their care and well-being, are strong, assertive, and looking out for them. These attitudes and actions are the cement that strengthens tribal bonds and activates our primitive social instincts.

On the surface, Clark violated nearly every rule of the kind and supportive tribal leader, but that was just on the surface. Tribal leaders need to respond in a variety of ways based on changing situations. While his methods would be totally out of place in a safe suburban school, they were a formula for success in a school that was riddled with violence and drugs. Thus, Clark is as much a preacher and a bouncer as he is a principal. He is a wartime leader who demands loyalty, discipline, and respect. Where Marva Collins preaches love, Clark says, "This is war!" The plaque on his desk reads, "I conquer circumstances."

The Power of Desire

Energy and persistence conquer all things.

Benjamin Franklin

The son of two Brazilian teachers, Jaime Escalante began teaching math at Los Angeles's Garfield High in 1974 (Escalante, 1990). He soon learned of the long-standing prejudices against his Mexican American students and their poor self-image as learners. The culture of East Los Angeles and the low morale at Garfield High painted a bleak picture of the future. Escalante preached to his students that only *ganas* (desire) was required to succeed—the moment-to-moment choice to work hard, persevere, and stand up in the face of adversity. He felt that his job was to bring out the *ganas* in each of his students. Escalante worked tirelessly, before and after school, on weekends, and during summers, alongside his students, never asking them to work harder than he worked himself.

Historically, a majority of Mexican American students have been considered "slow learners" or worse in American schools without regard for their lack of acculturation or English language skills. Contrary to these deeply ingrained prejudices, Escalante felt that all students perform up or down to the level of the expectations placed upon them. Because the only way out of their current lifestyles of gangs, violence, and poverty was hard work, he had to build their self-esteem while not cutting them too much slack. It was clear to Escalante that gangs leveraged the power of group identity and secure attachment in ways that educational systems largely ignore. He had to create a family that was more compelling and that allowed his students to escape the cycle of poverty and drugs for which many were headed.

Escalante's strategy was to be far more demanding than other teachers and to require each student to sign a contract to solidify their commitment to work harder and put in longer hours than their peers. To enter his classroom each day, students had to turn in their homework, which he called the "ticket to the show." Once inside, students found that they had entered the math Olympics, engaging in routine warm-ups where they would clap their hands and stomp their feet. His students wore special sports jackets, hats, and school T-shirts to psych them up to take exams. The hodgepodge of sports slang, pop culture, and high school vernacular that constituted the secret language of Escalante's class tribe made no sense to outsiders. They didn't need gangs outside of school because they were members of the Escalante tribe.

Under Escalante, his "unteachable" Mexican American students excelled on the nationally administered AP calculus test. Their performance was so good that the entire class was suspected of cheating and forced to retake the test under close scrutiny. With both their intelligence and integrity under suspicion, they dug deep and repeated their excellent performance a second time.

While respect, discipline, and hard work were pillars of his classroom, Escalante believed that "students learn better when they are having a good time." Over the years, he became part teacher and part entertainer, engaging his class with humor while using a variety of games to stimulate their interest and participation. He mixed jokes, card tricks, and games with quizzes, lectures, and memorization drills. He even held up a small clown head as a reminder that they would end up working at Jack in the Box if they didn't do their homework. Through a flair for the unexpected and his proclivity for showmanship and improvisation, Escalante made math engaging and fun.

Due to their age, ethnicity, and income, many of the students with the most difficulty learning are those at the bottom of the social hierarchy. Their struggle with multiple layers of disrespect on a daily basis makes the establishment of respect and empowerment in the classroom all the more vital. A tribal teacher like Escalante recognizes the power of love, interest, and a willingness to listen as central educational tools. When a student receives the same respect he is expected to give, he realizes that he is a worthy and valuable member of the class. All of these practices support the creation of secure attachment while activating primitive social instincts and the neuroplasticity of learning.

Escalante shaped his class into a tribe through a wide range of attachment-based practices. Like Joe Clark, he and his students faced the common enemies of poverty and prejudice in ways that solidified their bond. The battle against the calculus exam and the subsequent fight with the testing board further deepened their sense of tribe. In the process of this heroic struggle, Escalante guided his students to build new identities as warrior-learners; he provided them with both the model and the experience of hard work leading to success. This generates a revolutionary and heroic narrative in place of one shaped by the hopelessness and shame of internalized prejudice.

Escalante and other tribal chiefs gained authentic leadership through service and self-sacrifice. Mutual hard work, team spirit, and the secret language they shared supported group cohesion and a feeling of being a part of something both exclusive and special. His students formed a new gang with a strong leader and a shared goal of passing the big exam and attaining future success. Escalante's love of humor turned learning into play, decreased anxiety, and supported the neuroplastic mechanisms of new learning. As a tribal leader, he made sure that his students knew he believed in them and fought to instill within them the pride and courage they needed to succeed.

Escalante clearly recognized the power of relationships to change lives and realized that for some of his students, he was the first person to show them love. He was seen as a father figure and, like a father, he stood up for and stood up to many angry and troubled kids. He once asked his students what they wanted from their parents. They told him peace at home, understanding, trust, and love. In reflecting on his years of teaching, he realized that these were the values that he had always held in his heart.

Escalante demonstrated that creating common, worthy goals for our students helps to form and solidify tribal bonds, even in the face of gangs in the community. He also demonstrated the value of making your students feel safe and cared for. However, students also need to be challenged—affection is not a substitute for hard work, dedication, and desire. The take-home message from Escalante is to be yourself, bring your passion into your classroom, and don't be afraid to be a little silly. Our vulnerability is an invitation for our students to open up their hearts to us.

Pride and Passion

It is the mark of an educated mind to be able to entertain a thought without accepting it.

                                                            Aristotle

Biodiversity and individual diversity are among nature's strategies to ensure survival. We are all different from one another so that we can each contribute in our own way. A tribe consists of individuals with an array of skills and abilities as well as strengths and weaknesses. Arranging a mosaic of individuals to optimize performance is the job of a good tribal chief, sports coach, or any team working toward a common goal.

The fundamental nature of biodiversity may be a primary reason why the one-size-fits-all model of industrial education doesn't work for so many students. A broadly successful learning environment needs to contain a range of learning modalities and specialty areas that parallel the breadth of human diversity. This has to go much deeper than the traditional dichotomy of academic and commercial programs that emerged during the last century.

Not only is it unnatural and ineffective to teach the same material to all students in the same way, and at the same pace, but it can actually be damaging to many of the students' psyches and self-esteem. When a standard curriculum is presented in a fixed environment, the students for whom it is a bad match become either bored or ashamed; both get turned off to learning. When children are forced to read at times and in ways that they are not ready for, they experience shame instead of enjoyment and failure instead of accomplishment. Gifted children have a complementary problem with the stress of boredom. Learning can become a dreaded activity, and the experience of failure and indifference can generalize beyond the walls of the classroom. Democracy in the classroom helps alleviate these problems. When students can choose how they learn, they can choose methods that better suit their learning styles.

As discussed earlier, culture was shared and transmitted through stories for countless generations before written language. Narratives, from both literature and personal experience, are emotionally engaging, memorable, and contain lessons about every possible human challenge. In a very real sense, teaching through stories evokes the historical power of tribal elders and taps into a way of learning that our brains find most natural. Stories are also key for all of us in becoming more mindful and self-aware, allowing us to question the world around us and to create alternative narratives we can use to better regulate our emotions and guide our behaviors.

Following his own passion for exploration and facing new challenges, Rafe Esquith (2003, 2007) creates a classroom environment buzzing with life. Because he believes that children learn primarily by being exposed to new situations, Esquith fills each day with an orchestrated flow of stimulating challenges and exciting opportunities to learn. The constant newness is designed to capture and hold attention, enhance memory, and make learning dynamic, exciting, and fun.

His fifth graders move from task to task in thirty- to sixty-minute blocks from learning algebra, to playing rock and roll, to reading. Later in the day, they may engage in book binding, designing string art, or weaving carpets, before moving on to practicing for an upcoming math exam. Esquith's orientation to discipline is to make learning so interesting that the worst punishment is to be banned from participation.

On the first day of class, Esquith tells his students that his purpose is to guide them to explore their motivations, to think critically about issues of right and wrong, and to develop a personal code of behavior. He encourages his students to see each moment as an opportunity to develop character and evolve as a person. Like Albert Cullum, Esquith uses productions of Shakespeare to expose students to an array of human emotions, motivations, and behaviors. His goal is to present them with meaningful questions of values and ethics that lead them to different ways of understanding success.

Another core element of his teaching method is a system of microeconomics. Each student is assigned a job (banker, hall monitor, office messenger, clerk, and so on) for which they receive monthly paychecks, and they earn bonuses when they do extra work. Students pay rent on their desks, balance a checkbook, pay taxes, or suffer monetary consequences for being late or not doing their job. Purchases made with savings at the end of the school year reinforce the value of delayed gratification and hard work.

Because Esquith feels that books are doorways to lifelong learning, he is careful to make sure that each student has a positive reading experience. He plans each reading lesson by matching the right book to each student's interests and abilities and makes sure to provide the right scaffolding to ensure success. Through this kind of care, he hopes to instill a love of reading that encourages students to persevere in their learning. He teaches his students that "failure is not trying" and celebrates mistakes as opportunities to try again.

While attending college, a former student registered Esquith's class as a nonprofit organization and secured grants to support his work. The funds were used to buy audiovisual equipment to record the plays and musical performances and to go on field trips that most students were unable to afford. These field trips, earned through many hours of additional study, are integral to the curriculum. Before going to a Dodgers game, for example, students have to learn the rules and history of baseball and play a game themselves. For a trip to Washington, DC, students study about the Lincoln Memorial, review the inscription on the monument wall, and learn about the Civil War. Lessons about Native American culture are paired with camping trips to South Dakota, Montana, and Wyoming. Esquith's method of "going mobile" with his students stimulates their passion for exploration and brain networks dedicated to new learning.

Another aspect of trip preparation is teaching students about airplane travel, restaurant etiquette, and hotel procedures. He teaches organization, planning, and awareness of others by assigning roommates months in advance, providing diagrams of the hotel rooms so they know where to put their belongings, and he even has them coordinate their shower schedule. Esquith creates a matrix of experiences to build a sense of community that serves as a foundation for exploration and discovery.

Despite the fact that many of his students come from impoverished backgrounds or speak little English, his assumption is that they are all capable of success. Toward this end, he strives to make his classroom accessible to all learning levels, and he weaves the teaching of language skills into every lesson. Like the other educators we have discussed, Esquith places high expectations on his students in the belief that true excellence takes sacrifice, hard work, and enormous effort. Simultaneously, his methods help make it possible to build the confidence necessary to face new challenges, endure negative feedback, and overcome other obstacles to learning.

Esquith is a man on a mission, and his actions speak as loudly as his words. He spends twelve hours a day, six days a week, forty-eight weeks out of the year either in the classroom or offering free SAT classes on Saturdays for former students who are applying for college. He believes that kids do not mind having a hard teacher if the teacher is fair and holds himself to the same standards they expect. Beneath it all, Esquith's goal is to demonstrate how the classroom is like a family to which each member makes a variety of important contributions.

Tribal teachers like Esquith and Escalante fight for their students like father bears, willing to endure alienation, gossip, and naysayers in order to advocate for their tribes. The tribal teacher shapes the classroom into a secure base, and for students who lack this at home, a tribal classroom may be their best and last chance to have this experience.

Esquith demonstrates the importance of innovation, novelty, and flexibility in the classroom to accommodate the passions and needs of your particular students. And by chunking his lessons in briefer periods of time, he has found that students are better able to maintain attention, focus, and interest through the day. Esquith's work also demonstrates the importance of individualized teaching to each student, especially those who may be challenged in cognitive, social, and emotional functioning. In addition to his two books cited above, check the additional resources section at the back of this book for suggestions for bringing drama and microeconomics to your classroom. There are also ideas about sources of additional funding for classroom programs you may want to create.

CHAPTER 11

The Heroic Journey and the Quest for Wisdom

Do not lose courage in considering your own imperfections.

St. Francis de Sales

Although it is difficult to predict the exact knowledge and skills our students will need to succeed later in life, they all need to become the hero of their own story. We need to face our fears, push forward, and dare greatly if we are to have a fulfilling and successful life. As a central part of this journey, students need champions—adults who serve as guides through the sharing of concern, compassion, and wisdom. The attainment of wisdom—knowledge with relevance to important human experiences—should be a personal goal of every teacher, as well an educational goal for her students. Regardless of what the future brings, we will always need wise heroes.

On good days, I am grateful to be a teacher. On bad days, I struggle with self-doubt and fantasize about changing careers. The things we discover on these days, hidden behind the shadows of our own insecurities, test our spirit and forge our courage. When the going gets tough, it is the solidity of our inner worlds and the strength of our attachments that make the difference between success and failure, enthusiasm or burnout.

As novelists and screenwriters always say, conflict reveals character.

Although teaching fits the definition of a profession, it feels more like a calling. Perhaps this is because for most of our evolutionary history, successful teaching was a matter of life and death. The young had to learn for their survival and for the survival of the tribe. This may also be why tribal teaching can look like performance art, demon possession, or a state of frenzy. There is little doubt that a teacher's passion and excitement stimulate learning. Rafe Esquith (2007) calls us to teach as if our hair is on fire. Marva Collins (1992) tells us to teach as if "Jesus himself" were in the classroom. Our hard work and the love of what we do expose our students to the kind of effort it takes to succeed while demonstrating that they are worth the time and energy we invest in them.

We may not all have it within us to teach with burning hair or to coteach with Jesus. Some may even question the sanity of teachers who pour so much of their time and energy into their students. At the same time, successful teaching is always an exercise in vulnerability (Palmer, 1998). We long for our students' attention and enthusiasm, but we often feel rejected, angry, and depressed when they refuse to engage with us. In my own classes, I put myself on the line. I share my mistakes, imperfections, and shortcomings along with my passions, political beliefs, and pet peeves. Our vulnerability is an invitation to our students to be vulnerable and open to learning more about themselves and the world.

Vulnerability is often painful. As public figures, we are easy targets for the projection of the emotions of others. A college professor with whom I found a great deal of fault triggered negative emotions from my relationship with my father. When I look at my own teaching reviews, I am impressed by the number of students who think I am either the best or worst teacher they have ever had. I believe both of those reviews. Their reaction to us is all part of their growth process in dealing with the variety of people they will encounter and the memories (conscious and unconscious) that will be evoked. In the same way, parents and administrators take out their frustrations on us for long-standing personal, cultural, and institutional problems that are far beyond our control. (I sometimes wonder if the way teachers are treated is society's collective revenge for the shame experienced as children at the hands of authority.)

If they lack the ability to express their feelings directly, students will act out their fear, sadness, and shame through sabotage, attacks, and disruptive behaviors. Students will scoff at your naïveté, optimism, and dedication. They'll place bets on how long you will stay and compete with each other to break your spirit. In essence, they will do to you what has been done to them—all the while hoping you are strong enough to stand up to them, live up to your promises, and not abandon them. Your students need to know that you are going to stay because authority figures have abandoned them before.

Most teachers in these situations feel frustrated and hopeless, suffer a crisis of faith, and question whether they have what it takes to succeed. Many will require the kind of hero's journey discussed in Chapter 9. Instead of chasing a white whale or fighting dragons, tribal teachers fight the forces of their students' pain, the absurdities of the educational system, and our own fears of failure. Because the strength for this heroic battle comes from deep within, I echo the voices of educators who have called for self-exploration and personal growth to become central components of teacher training.

> **Reflection Box**
>
> Take a moment to reflect on your own personal, heroic journey. Stimulate your thinking by asking yourself three questions: (1) What fears have I pushed through in my life to reach important goals? (2) What fears continue to limit my growth? (3) Are there any challenges that I am presently avoiding because of fear?

Although most of us don't become teachers expecting to be heroes, many of us discover that this is precisely what is required to be successful. The basic elements of childhood that many of us take for granted, such as physical safety, secure attachments, and sane and loving parents, are in many cases absent. New teachers soon learn that without a solid emotional foundation, there is neither discipline in the classroom nor openness to learning. When children are neglected, unloved, and unsafe, the brain gets the message that adults are dangerous, and it shuts down input from anyone in authority. Some traumatized or neglected students will do anything they can to undermine a teacher.

The Journey

Cleverness is not wisdom.

Euripides

If tribal teachers are to succeed in challenging classrooms, they will need to take an inner journey of personal transformation during which they will break away from old beliefs and identities. In the process, new challenges will continue to emerge that will require finding new courage. Those who come out on the other side will have a new vision of what it means to be a teacher. They will discover deeper emotional certainty concerning their vision and the empowerment that comes with surviving a worthy challenge. Thus, it is not enough for us to make our students the heroes and heroines of their own stories; we each have to compose our own heroic narrative.

The path along this inner journey will include wrestling with the legacies of our own shame so that we may be better able to create a nonshaming tribal culture. Like parents, teachers walk a thin line between providing support and allowing students to confront adversity. For most of us, supporting our students is usually far easier than watching them struggle with failure, shame, and rejection. Our abilities to do this often highlight our own emotional limitations. Sitting with a child's negative feelings necessitates that we are able to feel and tolerate our own.

Our inner journey provides us with the ability to see beyond misbehavior to the emotions below the surface. This added perspective allows us to move beyond doling out punishment to understanding, attuning to, and healing the causes of suffering. We also have to gain enough confidence and security to remember how to play, have fun, and engage in the kind of self-care required to stay balanced and healthy. In the midst of our day-to-day lives, we have to reconnect with our mission and sense of purpose. There is nothing easy about this, which is one of the reasons why the journey is so difficult and so valuable.

Our brains react the same way to threats against our personal identity as they do to threats of physical harm. Because of this, disrespect, shame, and humiliation shut down learning like a fire alarm stops a class in its tracks. Attachment-based teachers do whatever it takes to minimize shame in interactions with their students and in students' interactions with one another. In an optimal learning environment, the same zero tolerance should be established for shaming as for bullying. Using fear, embarrassment, and shame to control students is a clear indication that we are not viewing the classroom from the eyes of our students. Like tribal chiefs, teachers' authority will come to be recognized and respected based on the respect and compassion they show their students.

In order to reach and teach a class, an attachment-based perspective calls on us to grasp the outer and inner worlds of our students. Students need to know their interests, passions, needs, and vulnerabilities are both felt and respected. Understanding the world from their point of view and striving to empathize with their philosophies and beliefs creates the possibility for an emotional attunement and helps them to "feel felt" by you.

Reflection Box

In Chapter 5, you remembered events from your childhood that caused shame. Now, take a moment to think back to a childhood experience of criticism that caused shame. Sit with the emotions it activates for about a minute. These memories will serve as a window to your students' experiences. Remember, having been a child only helps us to understand our students to the degree to which we remember how it actually felt.

Building secure attachments is the gateway to emotional regulation, self-esteem, and learning. Since the same factors that make a healthy home are present in a tribal classroom, it becomes an opportunity for reparenting and shaping new attachment experiences. Whether they are establishing consistency via norms, instilling the students with a curative sense of belonging, or unifying the class against a negative outside force, these teachers become loving and protective parents to their students. In turn, students become caring and supportive siblings to one another. This creates a safe haven and a secure base from which to explore, take risks, and build self-esteem as a valuable and valued individual.

Teaching Wisdom

A single conversation with a wise man is better than 10 years of study.

Chinese proverb

In small-scale societies, wise elders serve as the glue for their families and communities, and they are sought out for their knowledge, guidance, and comfort. By age and position, teachers are the wise elders of schools. Students will naturally want to turn to you for assistance, emotional support, and parental guidance. The attainment of wisdom and sharing your wisdom with others may be the social brain's greatest accomplishment and the ultimate goal of education.

As an expression of our social and emotional intelligence, wisdom requires sustained and caring connections with others that result in a deep sense of belonging. In the East, wisdom has traditionally focused on controlling one's thoughts, increasing self-awareness, and promoting social harmony. Wisdom in the Western world is seen as good advice, codes of social behavior, and more mystical knowledge related to the workings of heaven and earth. Increasing contact between East and West appears to have resulted in a blended view of wisdom as a combination of knowledge and compassion expressed through service to others. This is why maximum exposure to different people living in many different ways may be one of our best forms of education.

Knowledge and wisdom are related, yet separate abilities. While knowledge gives you the capacity to understand what you are doing, wisdom helps you to attain a correct, prudent, and just application of that knowledge. This is probably why knowledge can be judged against objective standards while wisdom is recognized in the heart and acknowledged through group consensus.

Who comes to mind when you think of a wise person? How about a caring grandfather, rabbi, minister, or guru? How about a public figure like a politician, scientist, or celebrity? When a group of undergraduates was asked to name well-known wise individuals, their top ten choices were as follows: (1) Gandhi, (2) Confucius, (3) Jesus, (4) Martin Luther King Jr., (5) Socrates, (6) Mother Teresa, (7) Solomon, (8) Buddha, (9) the Pope, and (10) Oprah Winfrey. The same question can be asked and explored in your classroom as a springboard for exploration of the concept and experience of wisdom.

Application Box

Who is wise? And what makes them wise? To stimulate a class discussion, ask students to write down or name a public figure and a person they think is wise. This will get students to learn more about each other while exploring the concept of wisdom. You can even play the "What would the wise person do" game by applying it to moral and ethical questions facing the students. If you want to push the limits a bit, you can ask students to name the wisest person at your school—although this could lead to some conflict. Finally, ask students to name one way in which they consider themselves to be wise.

You may notice that we don't see Napoleon, Einstein, or Donald Trump on this list, so power, intellect, and wealth aren't synonymous with wisdom for these undergraduates. Instead, those who were thought of as wise are known more for their insight, compassion, and courage. In fact, four of the first five people on this list died for their beliefs. This view of wisdom reflects the evolutionary shift from individual survival to the higher value of protecting family, tribe, and country.

Wisdom brings together intellectual and emotional intelligence in ways that maximize affiliation and compassion. The type of character that contributes to wisdom is one that is grounded in strong moral principles and possesses the courage to stand up for them in the face of danger. Attaining wisdom involves being able to see past the surface of things to deeper levels of meaning. Wise individuals also seem able to discard notions of a singular correct perspective and remain open to new learning. A good example of this attitude comes from Michelangelo who, in his ninth decade of life, had written above his studio door *Ancora Imparo* (I'm still learning). This might be a good sign for all of us to hang over our desks for all our students to see.

The social science research suggests that wisdom in adulthood coalesces from a complex pattern of personality variables, life experience, and inner growth. Those judged as wise have been found to excel in coping with existential issues and grasping the relativism of values. They also tend to have good social abilities and a rich internal life, and are open to new experiences. People with wisdom are capable of sustaining their focus on a problem, as they consider its multiple dimensions, meanings, and their personal responsibility in the matter at hand. Given that navigating complex and difficult relationships is one of life's most enduring challenges, much of wisdom is expressed in how people interact with and treat one another. Because the attainment of wisdom is a developmental process that begins in childhood, we can chart a course toward wisdom at any age. As a teacher, you can be a vital link in each students' journey.

The Maturation of Thought

It is always in season for the old to learn.

Aeschylus

For adolescents and young adults, learning means to quickly gather information, organize talking points, and move on to convincing others. Because younger people tend to assume the existence of a single valid answer, a final solution is quickly decided upon and energetically defended. Given that adolescents have been historically responsible for starting families, hunting, and fighting wars, this sort of impulsivity and quick decision making has a deep survival-based history. In my experience, preteens—not yet driven by neurological, emotional, and social upheaval—often seem much wiser than they will be in years to come.

The following list includes some of the factors typically found in the problem-solving strategies of early-stage thinkers:

Earlier-Stage Thinkers Demonstrate

- Rigidity and a need for certainty and control
- Black-and-white thinking and a limited recognition of life's complexity
- A lack of openness to the unconscious
- Less humor and empathy—more denial, blame, and projection

Adapted from Labouvie-Vief, 1990

The way adolescents and young adults think about problems is also tied to their primary developmental challenge of constructing a social identity. A central component in this process involves creating idealized mental images of the self. As the young person is confronted with new and more attractive options, each one is tried on, and, for a time, it feels like the final and best one. As part of their search for absolute truths, adolescents and young adults hold themselves and others to high standards tied to abstract ideals. Many use their identification with these ideals to remain free from blame, avoid disagreements, and place responsibility for problems on others.

All of these factors often lead adolescents to feelings of disappointment in their teachers and parents. I imagine this may sound familiar to those with adolescent children or with good memories for their own adolescence. I think it was Aristotle who first said that when he was sixteen, he was impressed by how dumb his father was. At twenty-five, his father was much brighter, and he was impressed with how much the old man had learned in just nine years.

It has been said that philosophy is born in seaports and trading centers. These are towns and cities that bring together people of different cultures, beliefs, and customs. It is this exposure to alternative worldviews that turbocharges the expansion of perspective. If you have a multicultural classroom, you have a seaport right in front of you. The knowledge contained in your students can be converted into wisdom through an exploration of similarities and differences between individuals and culture.

Application Box

Consider planting the seeds of wisdom by promoting aspects of mature thinking in every assignment and group project. Training in wisdom could include being encouraged to shift focus from specific details to general principles and broader perspectives. Experiences and classroom exercises that encourage an awareness of the complexity of human experience and the limits of human understanding also promote mature thinking. Push your students to take alternative perspectives and see things from the point of view of those they don't agree with.

While the answers to complex problems often seem obvious to adolescents, experience teaches us that solutions to human problems are hardly ever simple or straightforward and that not all of the important information may be immediately apparent. The accumulation of experience provides us with a framework that allows us to sit with ambiguity while we ponder complex problems. All of this higher-order mental processing depends upon emotional regulation, impulse control, and tolerance for ambiguity and uncertainty. Because thinking serves at the pleasure of emotion, it is certain that becoming wise depends upon emotional regulation. All of these aspects of the development of wisdom can be woven into every learning situation.

The following factors are typically found in later-stage thinkers:

Later-Stage Thinkers Demonstrate

- Flexibility of thinking and less concern with being in control
- Openness to the unconscious
- Tolerance—an ability to tolerate limitations and ignorance in self and others
- Increased empathy, compassion, and humor—less denial, blame, and projection

Adapted from Labouvie-Vief, 1990

Thanks to denial and our other psychological defenses, most of us are able to cope with the reality of our vulnerabilities and mortality. The lucky ones among us have the luxury of confronting these existential realities gradually and in small doses. As we grow older, however, we start to gain an increasing recognition and acceptance of our frailty and the inevitability of death. When people are traumatized, especially early in life, their defenses and assumptions of safety are shattered. The unfortunate reality of modern life is that child neglect is common; parents are either stressed or absent and violence is an everyday event. In fact the majority of children from inner cities know someone who has died a violent death.

While no one would choose to experience trauma, it has the potential to enhance self-discovery and support the attainment of wisdom. Think back to the list of the 10 wisest people mentioned earlier. Most of them found ways to transform their suffering into sources of wisdom. In fact, the central tenets of Buddhism are based on the belief that suffering is at the core of human existence. In order for this to occur, trauma and suffering need to be transformed by being provided both context and meaning. The work of Erin Gruwell and her Freedom Writers is a wonderful example of this process in action. If your students are suffering, they may benefit from these examples and from learning that they are not alone. Human suffering is universal.

Wisdom, Prejudice, and the Brain

The wisest of the wise may err.

Aeschylus

The near universality of racial prejudice seems to support the belief that we are hardwired to fear people who are different from ourselves. In the lives of our tribal ancestors, a rapid and automatic system to detect unfamiliar others would benefit us by avoiding potential attackers or exposure to new diseases. To whatever degree this scenario of natural selection holds true, it would make sense that contemporary racial prejudice would have its roots in our primitive fear circuitry.

To explore the social neuroscience of racial prejudice,

brain activation in Caucasians and African Americans has been compared while subjects were exposed to same- versus other-race faces. A clear same-race advantage in face recognition has been repeatedly demonstrated. Thus, Caucasians think about other Caucasians in far more complicated ways than they think about African Americans, resulting in much less conscious consideration. The statement "they all look alike" may reflect an underlying truth of how we deploy our attention when looking at other- versus same-race faces (Phelps, Cannistraci, & Cunningham, 2003).

It has been demonstrated that African Americans are better at recognizing Caucasian faces than vice versa, a phenomenon that is likely due to greater exposure to Caucasian faces in the media. We do know that through exposure and conscious attention to facial details, Caucasian adults come to successfully distinguish among African American faces. Interestingly, this learning process results in a decrease in implicit racial bias, suggesting that conscious attention and awareness decrease the amygdala activation and the fear that drive prejudice.

When pictures of well-known and well-liked African Americans were presented to Caucasian subjects, amygdala activation was absent. These results suggest that exposure to and knowledge about a person of a different race can teach the brain not to be afraid. Segregation seems to perpetuate and enhance prejudice by keeping our brains from learning about one another, leaving us to analyze the faces of people from other races with less efficient neural circuitry, and making us more vulnerable to cultural stereotypes and media representations.

Assuming that fear was at the heart of prejudice, a second line of research directly explored amygdala activation in same- and cross-race situations. It was found that when Caucasians and African Americans are shown pictures of other-race faces, they exhibit more amygdala activation compared to same-race faces. Although it takes approximately 500 milliseconds for a visual stimulus to reach conscious awareness, information about race is coded in just 50 milliseconds. This means that race influences our perception of a person before we are even consciously aware of seeing the person. The rapidity of this response also results in the automatic and instantaneous front-loading of our unconscious emotions and biases into the experience of each new person.

This fear activation influences our conscious experience in many ways. For example, individuals from other groups are more readily associated with danger. This is the likely reason why African Americans are more readily misperceived as carrying weapons and black faces are more likely to be perceived as angry by Caucasians. Other-race speakers are seen as more forceful or powerful than a same-race speaker. White students who rate higher in tests of social dominance actually perform better on tests administered by a black teacher, who presents an unconscious challenge to these white students.

Application Box

Although it can be uncomfortable talking about racism and prejudice, this research strongly suggests that open, honest, and respectful discourse about race is the best way to combat its negative effects. Because trust depends on honesty and transparency, it is difficult to achieve a tribal setting when biases among class members go unspoken and unresolved. How prejudice is discussed in a classroom will depend on you, your students, and the type of culture that you have created. Often, the best way to approach prejudice is to first invest time in studying races and cultures. The usual discovery is that beneath the superficial differences we are far more alike than different.

We know from studies of anxiety and fear that conscious labeling activates cortical neural networks that can regulate emotional activity. Talking about African Americans results in less amygdala activation in Caucasians, reflecting the ability of conscious processing to inhibit fear. In other words, people with low levels of stereotyping have learned to inhibit their automatic responses and replace them with thoughts and feelings more reflective of equality and empathy. Via conscious effort, they have disconnected reflexive prejudice from their behavior.

Social psychologists have found that stereotypes are automatically activated and require conscious inhibition to produce low-prejudice responses. Once stereotypical attitudes and beliefs are instilled, change requires intention, attention, and time. Because most children are exposed to some degree of racial prejudice, open discussion and increased interracial exposure work against prejudice. Increased awareness, focus, and exposure of the handicapped have also been found to decrease discrimination in the same way.

While racist practices and beliefs remain a current reality, we can actively work against their corrosive effects by supporting cultural pride, self-esteem, and increasing integration and contact between the races. Issues of race also have the potential of stimulating the kind of self-awareness and perspective that could enhance and promote the development of wisdom inside and outside of the classroom. A key lesson is that our willingness to communicate has to become stronger than our fear of being politically incorrect.

Exercise 10: Building a Tribal Classroom

Step 1: Creating an Awareness Plan

We were taught that a teacher's job is to transmit information, expand perspective, and teach students how to think. This is why so much emphasis is placed on creating teaching plans. Knowing our students as people and building relationships was a back-burner topic. The first step toward building a tribal classroom is to change these assumptions and realize that we have to put in the time and energy to learn how to connect, understand, and attach to our students. So we not only need a lesson plan, we also need a plan for awareness. In other words, what do we need to put in place to remind ourselves through-out the day to remember to pay attention to the people who are our students?

Step 2: Embrace Your Ignorance

The pressure to be perfect, know all the answers, and never make a mistake is a killer. It kills exploration, curiosity, and fun—three things we need to optimize learning. Perfectionism is born of shame and insecurity; most of us are conditioned early in life to push our failings and mistakes into the shadows. Our students know this about us, so when we ask them not to be afraid of mistakes, we are giving them a double message. My advice is to be ignorant, feel free to make mistakes, and reward your students for outshining you. If you allow yourself to be wrong, maybe they can too.

Step 3: Shuttling—Check in With Your Body, Heart, and History

One method that I use for increasing my awareness is something I call shuttling. By shuttling I mean a regular check on what I'm feeling and what I think is going on inside of those around me. If I find myself inside my head, I'll shuttle down into my body. If I'm caught or even lost in my feelings, I'll shuttle up to think about what may be happening.

If I'm feeling stuck or frustrated, I may pause for a moment and check in with myself to pay attention to what I'm feeling in my body or what images may come to mind. Ask yourself, what am I feeling in my body? What emotions am I experiencing? Does this remind me of something from my past? I often find that what I am not paying attention to is often more important than what I am focusing on. Perhaps I'm missing some important feeling in myself or someone else in the room. Being willing to share these inner processes or free associations often leads to fruitful discussions.

Step 4: Don't Freak Out—Use the Three A's Instead

A tribe needs to know their leader is level headed and competent when stressed. This ability to stay cool under pressure is especially important when a student discloses difficult experiences and feelings. Creating secure attachments and a proper holding environment requires the containment of challenging negative emotions. Don't confuse this with being unemotional. Attuning with difficult emotions is crucial; it is your ability to attune, absorb, and articulate these challenging feelings, that allows them to be transformed into social-emotional learning.

Step 5: Crisis Is Communication

We all act out from time to time. This is especially true for children and adolescents that lack the skills and abilities to become aware of, express, and work through difficult emotions. For the most part, we unenlightened humans react to someone else's acting-out with anger, fear, and an attempt to control or escape from them. A tribal chief will see beyond the acting-out to the emotions that drive it and engage with them instead of attempting to control the behaviors. This makes a child feel known and ultimately safe—although it may take time.

Step 6: The Gold Is in the Shadows

This is how Carl Jung described the fact that the things we most need to become aware of are those that our minds push out of consciousness. Tribal chiefs look to these shadows in themselves and their students and don't shy away from what they find. Shining light into the shadows can be transformative because it allows for conscious awareness and change.

Step 7: Practice RESETting

I was tutoring Antonio in math when he suddenly threw his book on the floor, called me an idiot, and put his head down on the desk.

Reflex.
Don't deny it—this happens, and it is important to expect it and get it under control. My initial reflex was to retaliate, and the words that came to mind were, "I'm giving up my free time

to help you and you have the nerve to call me an idiot! I'm the one who graduated from college; you're the one having trouble learning! To hell with you!" If you haven't already noticed, anger makes us stupid and more certain we are right.

Embracing my ignorance.

Fortunately, my awareness plan kept any of these words from escaping my lips; I took a few breaths and reminded myself that I was ignorant and that I didn't know what was going on inside Antonio. This time allowed me to ask myself the question, what is going on inside this young man?

Shuttling.

Shuttling down: My body felt very tense; I was feeling a lot of anger, and I felt very disconnected from Antonio. Shuttling up: I thought that perhaps I had been pushing him too hard and not paying enough attention to pacing and reinforcing his successes.

Empathy—attune, absorb, articulate.

I bet he was feeling really stressed. I know how that feels, and here is what I said: "I'm sorry I pushed you so hard. I got so caught up with how well you were doing that I forgot to pace you. You called me an idiot, and I'm wondering if that is how you felt because you had trouble with the last few problems." He looked up and stared at me for a while. "No one ever apologized to me for calling them an idiot before," he told me.

The gold is in the shadows.

After a few moments he added, "My father always called me an idiot when I made a mistake, and I hear his voice in my head every time I can't figure out the answer." This is gold because it articulates the unspoken background relationship that is playing out in the room. His father is in the shadow but still there with us, and Antonio often had a hard time telling me apart from his father.

CHAPTER 12

Higher Callings—
Deepening Experience

A loving heart is the truest wisdom.

Charles Dickens

A*s we conclude our exploration of attachment-based teaching, I would like to underscore the importance of two fundamental ideas. The first is the importance of deepening our human bonds by participating in worthy causes. The second is to become more centered, self-aware, and thoughtful about how we live our lives. Together these two goals reflect the two directions of relationship, our interconnection with others, and our relationship with our inner self. Woven together in our brains, minds, and spirits, inner and outer relationships bring us both to deeper inner experiences and to higher worldly causes.*

Our best guess is that humans lived in small family bands until about 12,000 years ago. Around that time, an "arms race" began and people began joining together into tribes of a few hundred. The strength of these larger groups led other groups to join together for survival. To up the ante, tribes later consolidated into chiefdoms, which were composed of thousands of individuals. Chiefdoms then had to join forces if they were to compete for land and resources. At the dawn of recorded history, chiefdoms had formed into the first city-states with tens of thousands of citizens. This sort of group consolidation continues to this day as nations form military and economic coalitions such as the North American Treaty Organization and the European Union.

As our social structures have undergone these rapid transitions, our brains have remained essentially the same. The success of nation-states, industry, and technology (and the general failure of smaller tribes) has led us to overlook the importance of our primitive social instincts. The same drives toward bonding, attachment, and loyalty are woven into our DNA. We are still guided by the primitive social instincts of blood relations that continue to be acted out in subgroups called combat units, gangs, and fraternity houses. While we can't go back to living in primitive tribes, we can strengthen our social connectivity in ways that allow us to live and learn better. A core component of a tribal group is sharing a common purpose or a worthy cause. This need is as fundamental for us as it was for our ancient ancestors.

Finding a Worthy Cause

Sometimes one man with courage is a majority.

Andrew Jackson

The most fundamental of all worthy causes, and the evolutionary origin of tribes, is the survival of those closest to us. For most of human evolution, and still to this day, people are unified by their need for food, shelter, and protection. The depth of this human motivation is seen whenever spontaneous tribes emerge in response to a threat to their survival. Banding together for the survival and well-being of others is a worthy cause with the deepest of evolutionary roots. By taking care of others, we ensure our own survival.

Sometimes a worthy cause already exists, and it is directly related to curriculum, grades, and academic advancement. For Jamie Escalante's students, success in school allowed an escape from a life of unemployment, poverty, and drugs. After the integrity of Escalante's students came under question, an additional mission was added—fighting the racial prejudice that dictated that Mexican American students can't learn. Erin Gruwell wove her students' fight for survival into the classroom by making their real-life struggles central to the curriculum. Children growing up in impoverished communities are faced with many real challenges and benefit from having something to fight for, especially when that cause is their own survival.

For most of you reading this book, day-to-day survival is probably a less immediate problem. Sadly, one of the costs of privilege is the loss of a built-in worthy cause. Without this, we have to search for something to give our lives meaning. Put in a slightly different way, we are designed not just to be social, but to struggle together to overcome obstacles. In other words, we are driven to become the heroes of the stories of our tribes. We all long to burn with passion, desire, and purpose, and the absence of meaning drives many to depression, despair, and suicide.

Because modern society has prolonged childhood to an almost absurd degree, most children and adolescents are not expected to take on any real responsibilities. Yet for most of history, childhood and adolescence included major responsibilities to the tribe. Without a worthy challenge, all of these energies are at risk of being channeled into fruitless emotional melodramas, video games, and tweets without end. Teenagers are in special need of worthy causes. We do them no favor by eliminating significant challenges from their lives.

Fortunately, it is easy to come up with a long list of worthy causes such as feeding the hungry, donating money to charities, or aiding in disaster relief. There is never a shortage of need: someone in the class with a sibling or parent fighting cancer; a trip to a sister school that is struggling to stay afloat; a classmate with a handicap who has difficulty navigating the school or seeing the board. These experiences, if close at hand, are more likely to activate an emotional response, which will help to propel recognition of the problem and the motivation to get to work. And while many schools support or even require community service, a mere assignment will not cement a tribe. To become a worthy cause, an assignment requires human contact to transform the cause from an abstract concept to real-life experience.

A central message of our tribal educators has been to challenge students to do great things. Most rise to the occasion, becoming empowered and building self-esteem in the process. And when students face a worthy challenge, they experience an additional benefit of feeling more deeply connected to others and their own sense of self. A wonderful Internet-based project for kids of all ages is to find another kid that tackled a big problem, inspired others, and made a difference. Sharing these stories can plant the seeds of all kinds of ideas for taking on worthy causes of our own.

Exploring Inner Space

Being entirely honest with oneself is a good exercise.
                                        Sigmund Freud

Because our brains evolved to navigate the physical world, reflecting on our inner thoughts and feelings doesn't come naturally. The Western focus on worldly activity and accomplishment makes us less likely to comprehend the idea of inner space. As society has sped up, there has been an increased demand for multitasking and processing external information with a parallel lack of focus on internal experience. Through exposure to practices like yoga and meditation, contact with Eastern cultures has helped those of us in the West to focus on inner experience and take the notions of mindfulness and awareness more seriously (Langer, 1997).

The path to developing self-awareness can be long and painful. In fact, it is usually when things are difficult or confusing that we tend to reflect on our inner experiences. But it doesn't always have to involve pain. For some, self-awareness involves prayer, for others self-analysis, and for others conversations with insightful friends and relatives. Meditation practices focus on becoming aware of your stream of consciousness or becoming more aware of bodily experiences.

Application Box: Creating Inner Space

A fun way to play with inner space is to start with an imagination game. Have each student chose the kind of space they would feel most comfortable and safe in—a tree house, a submarine, a castle are all possibilities. Have your students sit quietly with their eyes closed as you encourage them to furnish their inner space with furniture, chairs, books, snacks, and whatever else they like. Pause from time to time and encourage them to take slow, deep breaths to associate the pictures of their inner space with a relaxed body. Make sure to tell them that this inner space and the peaceful feelings associated with it are always inside them. Also, remind your students that they can come back to this space anytime they feel tense or afraid, or just need a break from the world. This exercise can also help children develop a way to talk about boundaries and alone versus together time, and supports emotional self-regulation by providing a visualization for self-soothing.

As you already know, I am particularly fond of teaching with stories, especially when they involve the growth of character. The growth of character usually involves reflecting on the self in the context of some challenge. A special favorite is Huckleberry Finn's nocturnal conflict with his conscience about whether or not to turn the runaway slave Jim over to his owner. In the process he has an inner debate between the values he has been raised with and his human experience of his friend. Huck's inner struggle is great for stimulating discussions and for building a model for self-reflection. Here is a story of my own that you may want to use. Edit freely in any way you think might be helpful to your class.

One of my earliest memories of my relationship with my self and the benefits of self-reflection happened while I was in the eighth grade. I wasn't the best student, but I always enjoyed math and was good at it relative to other subjects. I had done well in seventh grade and continued through the first half of the eighth grade. Through the fall of eighth grade, my teacher grew larger and larger with her first child until she informed us that she would not be returning in January. When we returned after New Year's Day, a very young man with thick glasses and a bow tie sat at the front of the room. We were all sad that our beloved teacher was gone, but that was the least of our problems. This newly minted PhD, while likely very proficient in high-level theoretical mathematics, had no training as a teacher of middle school kids.

I soon discovered that my math abilities were highly dependent on the abilities of my teacher. In the following months, my grades slid from A to D, and I began calculating how many points I needed on the final to even pass the class. My meetings for extra help were not helpful, and he appeared irritated with my inability to understand his explanations. I suspect he felt as incompetent as a middle school teacher as I did as a student. I soon gave up on these meetings, and my requests to my counselor for tutoring went unanswered. I finally went back to my seventh grade teacher, who had both sympathy for my situation and a few hours after school to help me out. With his help, I studied for the final with every free moment and handed in the final exam optimistic about getting enough points to graduate to the next grade.

The following Monday, I was called into my counselor's office after lunch for a meeting. When I arrived, my math teacher and the principal were sitting with my counselor, all with somber looks on their faces. While, as you can imagine, this setting made me immediately uneasy, I could not imagine what was happening. I was a pretty obedient and anxious kid who wanted to please adults, so I didn't have experience being sent to the principal's office. They invited me to sit down across from them, which I did, and awaited my fate.

They began by telling me that they were trying to decide what to do because I had not handed in my math final the preceding week. It took me a while to grasp what they were referring to. When what they were saying finally registered, my heart started to race. I thought back to the exam, and I remembered walking up to the front of the room and putting the test in a box on the teacher's desk. I went through the memory step-by-step a couple times in an effort to make sure that I really did hand it in—after all, three adults were telling me that I hadn't. I knew I didn't leave it on my desk, and I knew it wasn't in my backpack, so I must have handed it in. I finally spoke up and told them that I did hand it in and explained how hard I had studied, that I had gotten help from another teacher, and that I thought I had passed.

They remained expressionless and my counselor told me that I had been doing poorly in the class, that my grades had consistently declined since January, and that my teacher felt that I didn't hand in the test because I knew I would fail. It was clear that I had been accused and found guilty before I arrived and my denial or any argument I presented were already too late. I sat with my head hung low, elbows on my knees, looking down at the black-and-white institutional floor tiles of the 1960s. While I felt concerned about my math grade, my eyes filled with tears from the shame and humiliation of not being believed. Being bad in math was a relatively minor problem, but being seen as a liar felt devastating. Being raised as a good Italian boy, little value was placed on academic success in my family but a great deal of weight was placed on honesty and integrity.

As I sat there watching my tears drop to the floor, I had the moment of self-reflection (which is the reason I'm telling you this story) that I mentioned before. I realized that anything I said would be heard as a lie and that I wouldn't be able to convince these three adults, who were already convinced of my guilt, that I had taken the test and handed it in.

A dawning awareness welled up from within me: I would be the only one who knew the truth and that would have to be enough. I had to stop pleading my case, get a hold of my emotions, and begin to negotiate a solution. My relationship with myself, and my ability to engage in an inner dialogue, were graduating from a figment of my imagination to a useful ally. Without it, I would have had no option but to become hysterical, lashing out or creating some complex conspiracy theory. Even worse, I could have become demoralized, depressed, and given up on school. This happens all too often, especially with insecurely attached children and adolescents who see teachers and principals as additional sources of shame and indifference.

In case you're curious, I ended up retaking the test and doing well, after which my first exam was discovered behind a storage cabinet. While I did learn a little math that year, the important lesson was the power of having a relationship with myself and an appreciation of self-awareness and inner dialogue as a powerful resource.

My math teacher the following year looked nothing like a mathematician. Sam Sherman was a short and stocky middle-aged man who sold nylons out of the trunk of his car on weekends. I never saw him without a cigar in his hand and a smile on his face. He was a great teacher who loved math and loved me, and I loved him back. There was no doubt in his mind that he would be able to teach me and that I would be able to learn. Failure wasn't an option for either of us, and letting him down was unacceptable. With his help and encouragement, I received a perfect score on the statewide math exam a year to the day after the meeting I described above. Sometimes only we know the truth, and that's all that matters.

First Steps to Understanding Our Inner Worlds

Although we need to go deep into our evolutionary history to understand our social instincts, we also need to use the abilities of our minds that have deepened more recently. Unlike primitive instincts that are automatic and unconsciously driven, self-awareness takes motivation, effort, and practice. Although most people pay almost no attention to their inner worlds, meditation and other self-reflective practices have been studied and explored for thousands of years. Although historically explored in the context of religious and spiritual pursuits, the notion of being self-aware, or "mindful," is beginning to be seen as an important aspect of everyday life.

We are discovering what many cultures already know; the relationship with the self is a way of carrying on internal conversations that contribute to our abilities to regulate our emotions, solve problems, increase perspective, and gain resilience. While there are many forms of meditation and many paths to self-awareness, you can begin to explore this with very young students by talking about the various voices they hear in their heads—the voice that tells them to take another cookie and the other voice that warns them they will get in trouble if anyone finds out. There are also voices that say bad things about them. As a class, you can explore where these negative voices come from and how to fight against them.

In exploring our inner worlds, we come to learn that our minds use language in different ways. In fact, through self-reflection, most of us become aware that we seem to shift among different perspectives, emotional states, and types of self-talk. You can support an expansion of self-awareness and emotional regulation by guiding students to become aware of these different kinds of internal languages and states of mind.

Learning that we are more than the voices that haunt us can provide hope and serve as a means of changing our lives. As the language of self-awareness is expanded and reinforced, we learn we are capable of evaluating and choosing whether to bow to our habits or follow the expectations of others. Keep in mind that self-exploration can be unnerving for the beginner, triggering confusing thoughts and uncomfortable feelings. Thus, it is important to prepare students by providing a context and a variety of mediums through which their experiences can be understood, expressed, and communicated to others.

Species Consciousness

One planet, one experiment.

E. O. Wilson

Why are passion and compassion the bedrock of successful teaching? The most basic answer is that all of us need the same thing—to be loved and appreciated, and to contribute to the good of others. This is what Jamie Escalante's students told him they needed most in life—peace at home, understanding, trust, and love. Families, tribes, classrooms, in fact, every human group can trace its origins back to nature's first experiments with bonding and attachment. As human beings, we need to connect with our students as much as they need to connect with us.

Children need a safe haven from which to meet the challenges of life. They also need a proper holding environment in which they can learn to cope with their inner struggles and the ups and downs of relationships. Without this, their minds and brains are closed to learning and the energy and resources poured into teaching fall on closed ears and shuttered brains. By watching a teacher work to create a cohesive tribe in the classroom, students get to witness what real heroism looks like.

Where are we headed and what are the most important goals of education? My best guess is that we are moving to a point in human history when our ongoing survival as a species will depend upon deeper attunement, enhanced empathic skills, and expanded communication. The combination of rapid population growth and worldwide communication is moving us toward the creation of a single tribe on a planet with diminishing resources and a compromised ecosystem. If education is simply a means to more consumption, competition, and militarization, we are sealing our own fate. On the other hand, if we can develop a sense of connectedness to all humanity and become good stewards of our planet, we have a chance. I would call anything that furthers this goal good education.

The interdependence of our relationship with ourselves and our connection with others are achievements that are like two facets of the same diamond. On the one hand, our ability to have a rich inner life depends upon having a trusting connection with others and the world around us. On the other hand, our ability to connect deeply with others relies on self-awareness, acceptance, and inner peace. Building a secure tribal classroom, combating shame, and expanding self-awareness are the central goals of this book.

Exercises

Exercise 1: Going Tribal

Exercise 1 discusses the basics of creating a tribal classroom. Teachers can utilize this exercise to start discussions with their students. As a group, the class can determine which aspects of a tribal classroom will facilitate learning. Exercise 1 also addresses the concept of classroom contracts that establish everyone's responsibilities to the tribe.

Exercise 2: Roadblocks to Learning

In Exercise 2, teachers can explore student experiences that have hindered learning in the past. This opportunity allows everyone to understand what techniques will not work for their students. Teachers may also learn about trauma that has occurred in previous academic settings.

Exercise 3: Caring for Ourselves and Our Tribe

Teachers can utilize Exercise 3 to gain more insight into students' personal experiences with stress and anxiety. Exercise 3 also focuses on the coping strategies that students currently employ when stressed. As a class, everyone can determine which coping mechanisms will be utilized when difficult situations come up in the classroom.

Exercise 4: Learning to Chill

Exercise 4 focuses on helping students and teachers to assess their anxiety and use techniques to reduce classroom stress.

Exercise 5: Understanding and Combating Shame

Exercise 5 addresses how students perceive failure, shame, and the lasting effects of shame. Teachers can also utilize Exercise 5 to reduce shaming experiences in the classroom. It also discusses techniques that can fight shame that students bring into the classroom from previous experiences.

Exercise 6: Teacher Self-Assessment— Am I Being Bullied?

In Exercise 6, teachers have the opportunity to assess their current work environment. Teachers can use this exercise to determine how they feel about their students, their administration, and their personal experience as a teacher. If a teacher does feel bullied or burned out, it will affect every facet of his or her life.

Exercise 7: Exercising Empathy

Teachers can use Exercise 7 to inspire more empathy in their students. This exercise allows students to understand what it really means to be heard and understood. Students can also discuss what make them feel listened to. The exercise also helps students differentiate between empathy and sympathy.

Exercise 8: Into the Unknown

Exercise 8 focuses on how novelty can be used to reach students. This exercise includes some small-scale activities that can introduce novelty in the classroom. Exercise 8 also addresses some of the anxiety that can be caused by new things or situations.

Exercise 9: Writing Your Own Story

Teachers can utilize Exercise 9 to help students write their personal stories. Writing a self-narrative will allow students to address past traumas, to become more active in their own lives, and to inspire new hopes and goals for the future.

Exercise 10: Building a Tribal Classroom

Exercise 10 provides an overview for teachers, addressing the various steps involved in building a tribal classroom. It focuses on creating a plan, understanding your limitations, being self-aware, and remaining calm.

References

Bowlby, J. (1988). *A secure base*. New York: Basic Books.

Brown, B. (2012). *Daring greatly*. New York: Gotham.

Campbell, J. (1968). *The hero with a thousand faces (Bollingen Series, No. 17)*. Princeton, NJ: Princeton University Press.

Clark, J. (1989). *Laying down the law: Joe Clark's strategy for saving our schools*. Washington, DC: Regnery.

Collins, M. (1992). *Ordinary children, extraordinary teachers*. Newburyport, MA: Hampton Roads.

Escalante, J. (1990). The Jaime Escalante math program. *The Journal of Negro Education, 59*(3), 407–423.

Esquith, R. (2003). *There are no shortcuts*. New York: Anchor.

Esquith, R. (2007). *Teach like your hair is on fire*. New York: Penguin.

Filipovic, Z. (2006). *Zlata's diary: A child's life in Sarajevo*. New York: Penguin.

Freedom Writers, with Gruwell, E. (2007). *The Freedom Writers diary: How a teacher and 150 teens used writing to change themselves and the world around them*. New York: Broadway.

Ginott, H. (1972). *Teacher and child: A book for parents and teachers*. New York: Macmillan.

Gruwell, E. (2007). *Teach with your heart: Lessons I learned from the freedom writers: A memoir*. New York: Broadway.

Hoff, S. (2000). *Oliver (I can read series: Level 1)*. New York: Harper Collins.

Kaufman, G. (1974). The meaning of shame: Toward a self-affirming identity. *Journal of Counseling Psychology, 21*(6), 568–574.

Labouvie-Vief, G. (1990). Wisdom as integrated thought: Historical and developmental perspectives. In R. J. Sternberg (Ed.), *Wis-*

dom: Its nature, origins, and development (pp. 52–83). New York: Cambridge University Press.

Langer, S. (1997). *The power of mindful learning.* Reading, MA: Addison-Wesley.

Meier, D. (2002). *The power of their ideas: Lessons for America from a small school in Harlem.* Boston: Beacon.

Palmer, P. (1998). *The courage to teach: Exploring the inner landscape of a teacher's life.* San Francisco, CA: Jossey-Bass.

Phelps, E. A., Cannistraci, C. J., & Cunningham, W. A. (2003). Intact performance on an indirect measure of race bias following amygdala damage. *Neuropsychologia, 41*(2), 203–208.

Pogrow, S. (2009). *Teaching content outrageously: How to captivate all students and accelerate learning.* San Francisco, CA: Jossey-Bass.

Potter-Efron, R., & Potter-Efron, P. (1989). *Letting go of shame: Understanding how shame affects your life.* New York: Hazelden.

Richerson, P. J., & Boyd, R. (2006). *Not by genes alone: How culture transformed human evolution.* Chicago, IL: University of Chicago Press.

White, M. (2007). *Maps of Narrative Practice.* New York: Norton.

Winick, M., Katchadurian, K., & Harris, R. C. (1975). Malnutrition and environmental enrichment by early adoption. *Science, 190,* 1173–1175.

Yerkes, R. M., & Dodson, J. D. (1908). The relation of strength of stimulus to rapidity of habit formation. *Journal of Comparative and Neurological Psychology, 18,* 459–482.

Zull, J. (2002). *The art of changing the brain. Enriching the practice of teaching by exploring the biology of learning.* Sterling, VA: Stylus.

Suggested Reading

Brown, B. (2012). *Daring greatly*. New York: Gotham.

Cozolino, L. (2006). *The neuroscience of human relationships*. New York: Norton.

Cozolino, L. (2013). *The social neuroscience of education*. New York: Norton.

Gilligan, C. (1993). *In a different voice: Psychological theory and women's development*. Cambridge, MA: Harvard University Press.

Heifetz, R. (1998). *Leadership without easy answers*. Cambridge, MA: Harvard University Press.

Miller, A. (1981). *Prisoners of childhood: The drama of the gifted child and the search for the true self*. New York: Basic Books.

Miller, A. (1983). *For your own good: Hidden cruelty in child rearing and the roots of violence*. New York: Farrar, Straus and Giroux.

Wilson, E. O. (2013). *The social conquest of earth*. New York: Liveright.

Additional Resources

Chapter One

Take a moment to watch Rita Pierson's inspiring TED talk, "Every Child Needs a Champion," to see a wonderful expression of opening closed minds with open hearts (http://www.youtube.com/watch?v=SFnMTHhKdkw).

Chapter Five

Please see an excellent TED talk by Dr. Brené Brown called "The Power of Vulnerability" (http://www.youtube.com/watch?v=iCvmsMzlF7o).

Chapter Six

Team-building exercises for elementary-age students can be found at http://ethemes.missouri.edu/themes/1045 and http://teambuildingactivitieshq.com/team-building-activities-for-kids/.

You may also want to have a look at *Reaching All by Creating Tribes Learning Communities* by Jeanne Gibbs, self-published by Center Source Systems in 2006.

Contact FuelEd Schools at http://fueledschools.com/wordpress/.

Chapter Eight

Teaching Content Outrageously by Stanley Pogrow (2009) describes the value of using the elements of drama, costume, and physical action while providing numerous examples of how to make material more human, emotionally impactful, and memorable. There is really nothing outrageous at all about this approach, but it does appear outrageous in contrast to a prototypical, orderly classroom. Pogrow is simply using the way our brains evolved to learn to enhance the classroom experience and optimize plasticity.

A Touch of Greatness (2004) is a must-see film for anyone who has ever spent any time as a child. Available through First Run Features (www.firstrunfeatures.com), it toggles back and forth between 1960s black-and-white footage of his class and more contemporary interviews of Mr. Cullum and his students as grown-ups reflecting on their experiences in his class.

Chapter Nine

And if you think this is only a boy's story, see the movie *Brave* or read Carol Gilligan's (1993) *In a Different Voice.*

The story of Erin Gruwell and her students was dramatized in the Hollywood film *Freedom Writers* (2007) and is available on DVD from Paramount Pictures. While romanticized and glamorized in order to earn money at the box office, it remains close enough to real life to make it an inspiring film for both teachers and students.

Chapter Ten

I recommend you see the documentary *Waiting for Superman* (2010), which includes interviews and commentary from Geoffrey Canada about the Harlem Children's Zone and the state of public education. It won the award for best documentary at the Sundance Film Festival and was named best documentary by the National Board of Review. Released around the same time, *The Lottery* (2010) and *The Cartel* (2009) both focus on the failures and hopes of education: they are also interesting and worth watching.

If you need a shot of inspiration, watch *Stand and Deliver*, the film based on Escalante's life and work.

Be sure to see Morgan Freeman as Joe Clark in the movie *Lean on Me* (1989) and check out John Stossel's interview with Clark on CBS's *60 Minutes* as well as Stossel's documentary, *Stupid in America*, at http://www.youtube.com/watch?v=Bx4pN -aiofw.

The Hobart Shakespeareans (2006) is a wonderful documentary about Rafe Esquith, his students, and their work together. Available through POV films (www.pbs.org/pov/hobart), it is a treasury of practical suggestions about creating stimulating educational experiences, classroom management, and teaching outside of the box.

Suggestions for Reaching Outside the Classroom

Among the unique characteristics of Rafe Esquith's class are the use of programs in microeconomics and drama and the availability of additional resources through external funding. If any or all of these ideas interest you, consider seeking to include them in your own classes. Besides Rafe Esquith's books as a source of ideas and inspiration, look into some of the following.

Microeconomics

While establishing a classroom economy may not be in line with your academic goals and other responsibilities, a volunteer organization called Junior Achievement (JA) may be able to help you expand learning outside the classroom. The goal of JA is to "foster work-readiness, entrepreneurship and financial literacy skills, and use experiential learning to inspire students to dream big and reach their potential." JA has organizations in most major cities and may serve as a valuable classroom resource. See https://www.juniorachievement.org/web/ja-usa/home for more details.

One of their programs, Junior Achievement BizTown, gives fifth and sixth graders the opportunity to run a town for a day. After extensive presite preparation, they perform jobs such as mayor, IRS agent, bank teller, and shop owner and actively participate in the economy and governance of the town. They learn how to write checks, take out a loan, and invest in a business while learning general lessons about the functions and functioning of the economy. To see how this works, watch http://www.youtube.com/watch?v=43PCCTwi3GA.

Drama

With the motto "Make the drama, don't become the drama," Harry Dawse offers tools and tips on how to guide a successful student production (http://www.drama-teaching.com/index .html).

Also see TeacherVision resources for drama (http://www .teachervision.com/drama/teacher-resources/55277.html).

Additional Classroom Funding

If you require additional classroom resources to implement programs, enhance technology, or take your students on field trips, consider investing some time in exploring outside funding. Here are three possibilities:

- Adopt a Classroom has a mission statement that is short and very sweet: "We connect donors with teachers to be classroom champions" (http://www.adoptaclassroom. org/teachers/teachers_landing.aspx).
- Donors Choose allows teachers to post classroom projects for donation requests, and donors will make contributions. When the request is fully funded, Donors Choose delivers the supplies or money to the teacher. The class then sends letters and photos to the site to provide feedback to the donors. Check it out at http://www. donorschoose.org.
- For a more general exploration of organizations that may be able to provide assistance to classroom projects, investigate the Foundation Center (http://foundation-center.org).

Chapter Eleven

One suggestion for a high school class would be to distribute, read, and discuss President Obama's short speech concerning the Trayvon Martin case and the Zimmerman trial in July 2013. I would begin by discussing the circumstances of Trayvon Martin's death and the issues that were raised during the court case. Here is the final line of the speech to provide you a little inspiration: "We should also have confidence that kids these days have more sense than we did back then, and certainly more than our parents did or our grandparents did; and that along this long, difficult journey, we're becoming a more perfect union—not a perfect union, but a more perfect union." Find the entire speech at http://www.huffingtonpost.com/ 2013/07/19/obama-trayvon-martin-speech-transcript_n_362 4884.html.

Chapter Twelve

Kiva is an international microeconomics resource where classes can become involved in helping small business around the world. A class can set up an account with donated or collected money and choose from among scores of requests for funding assistance from entrepreneurs around the world. It is not only a great way to help others, but can provide a real-life connection to lessons focused on economics, culture, and ethics. Find out more at http://www.kiva.org/lend?gclid=CNahhp-d6roCF adcMgodS0AA3A.

Explore the website GenerationOn to see hundreds of ways for kids to make the world a better place http://www.generation on.org/kids and visit Listverse for examples to inspire your students (http://listverse.com/2008/07/16/7-children-who-changed -the-world/).

Index

Note: Italicized page locators indicate illustrations; tables are noted with a *t.*